LOVE

LOVE

A SCIENTIFIC AND LIVING
PHILOSOPHY OF LOVE AND SEX

BY

Lao Russell

PUBLISHED BY
UNIVERSITY OF SCIENCE AND PHILOSOPHY
SWANNANOA, WAYNESBORO, VIRGINIA

PRINTED IN THE UNITED STATES OF AMERICA

Dedicated to the Youth of the World so that through their greater understanding of the Sex Principle, and of their oneness with each other, a new era of peace on earth shall come to pass.

Table of Contents

PART I

CHAPTER I—LOVE'S PHANTASY

CHAPTER II—HOW TO ATTRACT ROMANCE

The Qualities Which Attract	7
When You Create Beauty, You Express Romance	9
The Beauty Which Comes with Maturity	11
Everyone Appreciates Art	12
We Earn Love and Romance	13
Discipline with Love	15
Character Building in Early Youth	16
Live Love	18
The Fallacy of the Age Question	19
The Great Importance of Respect	21
Those Important Twenty-Three Hours	22

CHAPTER III—VICTORY OVER GUILT AND FRUSTRATIONS

Many Problems Created by Misunderstandings	24

Table of Contents

Overcoming Self-Condemnation	25
The Danger of Gossip	27
Our Greatest Challenge	29
Compromise Delays Fulfillment	30
From All That Is Unlovely Turn Thine Eyes	34
Television—Escape from Reality	34
A Temporary Sedative	35
The Great Opportunity of TV and Radio	38
What Is Your Secret Desire to Create?	43
Boys' and Girls' Clubs	45
To Create Is to Live	46
Alcoholism, Narcotics and Sex Excesses	47
Selflessness	49
Nature Thrills and Heals	49
All Living Things Respond to Love	51
The Emotion of Self-Reproach	52
A Teen-Ager's Great Victory	53
The Miracle of Love	56
Love's Victory	63
Now Is Eternity	63
Your Nightly Reborning	65

CHAPTER IV—THE MAGIC POWER OF SEX

Our Sex Drives	69
Every Interchange Is a Sex Interchange	71
The Effects of Sex Practices	71
Boy and Girl Sex	73
Time Element for Marriage	73

Table of Contents

The Qualities We Desire 75
Beauty Attracts 76
The Qualities the World Is Crying For 76
Suicide, Crime and Sex Unbalance 76
You Can Become a Human Dynamo 79
The Type of Mate for You 79
As We Start the Day 81
The Environment You Create 83
Sex Sublimation 84
The Magic Power of Sex 87

CHAPTER V—WHY MANY TEEN-AGE MARRIAGES FAIL

The Importance of Time 89
The Sex Impulse 91
Everyone Has to Make Adjustments 91
Heart to Heart Talks Can Save a Marriage 92
Balance Is the Key to Married Bliss 95
Know You Never Work Alone 98
True Love Is Forever 100

CHAPTER VI—THE SECRET OF HOLDING ROMANCE

Mutual Interests 101
The Agony of Unbalance 105
Knowledge Alone Controls Your Destiny 107

Table of Contents

The Great Need for Sex Knowledge   109
The Great Importance of Balanced Mating   110

CHAPTER VII—TRUE LOVE

Love Forevermore   114
Our Eternal Search for Love   115
How to Find That Perfect Love   116
Understanding What Motivates You   117
The Spirit of Christmas   118
What Is True Love?   121
True Love   123
Eight Color Photographs   125-132

PART II

CHAPTER VIII—THE VITAL ROLE OF TODAY'S YOUTH

Man's Self-Created Tensions   135
The Solution Lies in Knowing Cause   136
In Truth Is Freedom   138
The Law of Balance in Action   140
Country Life   141
Balanced Giving—Unbalanced Taking   143
The Law of Cause and Effect   144
The Inviolate Law of Rhythmic Balanced
    Interchange   144
The Basic Root of a Balanced Civilization   145
The Unlearned Lessons of Man   146
Nature Never Bargains. Nature Balances   148
Higher Sex Knowledge   149

Our New Age   151
Comprehending Our Oneness   153
Our Interdependence   155
You Can Give Birth to an Age of Char-
    acter   156
Your Desires Create Your Destiny   158
Code of Ethics   160
The Drama of the Play of Creation   161
The Agony of Man's Awaiting   161

CHAPTER IX—ON BUILDING A BRIGHT NEW AGE OF CHARACTER

The University of Science and Philosophy   167
World's Great Necessity   168
Walter Russell—the Man Who Tapped the
    Secrets of the Universe   169
Foretold the Calamities from the Use of
    Atomic Fission   170
Our United Purpose   171
Lao Russell   171
Forgetting Self   176
Courage to Do What Is Right   178
The Revolt of Nature   179
We All Need Each Other   181
Youth's Great Challenge to Create a New
    Age of Character   182
Finale   184
Eight Black and White Photographs   185-192

PART III

CHAPTER X—INTERNATIONAL AGE OF CHARACTER CLUBS

Need for Growth into Cultural and Sports
    Activities   196
Everyone Can Do Something   197
A Special Message to Our Students   197
Social Gatherings and Lectures   198
Students' Christmas Gatherings At Swan-
    nanoa   198
Wedding Bells   202
Pledge for Membership   204
Your Love Bank   205
A Letter from Me to You   206

Introduction
by
Walter Russell

It is difficult to portray so extraordinary a woman as Lao Russell because the standards usually applied to the average human do not apply to either the genius or illuminate type, or the super-intellectual to which she belongs. The very thinking of these rare inspired creators of the world's enduring culture is so diametrically opposite to that of the normal average person that the superior one is quite generally looked upon as inferior or even subnormal. Very often a schoolteacher misjudges a genius as being mentally subnormal and advises the parents to send him or her to a school for subnormals.

This difference in thinking which distinctly elevates the genius or illuminate into a transcendent thinker, as compared with the average man, can best be described as the difference between one who thinks inwardly toward the seat of intelligence and the masses who think outwardly through their senses. Because of this fact the super-thinker gains his knowledge cosmically and the average thinker gains it through observation and deductive reasoning. That is the reason why the world's super-thinkers often appear dull to those who gain their knowledge from books or by sensed observation.

Lao Russell is one of that rare type of transcendent thinkers of inner vision who has been enabled to manifest the super-power of the creative thinker because of her ability to gain knowledge cosmically. Everything which she says in her conversations with other people, or in her talks to groups, or in the books she writes, or in her teachings in the immortal Home Study Course she has written with me, is as different from the usual language of the masses as Shakespeare's writings differed from the writers of his day, or as Beethoven's music differed from the mass-produced music of this age.

Thousands of people of many countries all over the world have recognized this quality in her and have told her that she has made them think and talk differently because of it. When one views the crowning achievement of her life in the founding of a world University, with its student body in practically every country on the globe, in which to spread our teachings to those increasing numbers of people who have become ready and eager for higher knowledge of their relation to God, one realizes that only an extraordinary person could have accomplished such a miracle.

God awareness is the dominant characteristic of all illuminates but to Lao Russell it is as natural as her breathing. In her immortal book, *God Will Work With You But Not For You,* she clarifies this quality which characterizes highly advanced humans so clearly that many have written her that for the first time in their lives they now understand what the greatest of Illuminates of all time meant when He said, "I and my Father are ONE."

This fact accounts for her own self-education. Except for the basic physical information relating to such subjects as geography, reading, writing, and arithmetic, she needed no schooling. She was further ahead in these studies before she ever had a tutor. She could read and write better at three years of age than the usual child of eight or ten. At seven years of age she wrote fairy stories of publishable quality and taught herself to paint pictures in water color by the time she was ten which were of such merit that she sold many of them.

At three years of age Lao Russell first became aware that she was being prepared for the playing of a great role in human destiny. Its meaning was dim at that time but sufficiently clear to her that she often told her dolls that she had to grow up and save the world from destroying itself. As the years passed, this knowledge increased in definiteness to such an extent that she knew she was to fulfill her-Self and world destiny with another who was in America. This knowledge grew so strong in her that she tried the impossible feat of going to America at seventeen.

Introduction

The story of her many years of preparation for contributing to the transcendency of man, by giving her part of the new knowledge contained in the writings and teachings of the curriculum which distinguishes the University she has founded from all other universities, would fill many books.

I can but say of her in this brief review that her destiny set her apart from the routine of life and took her to all parts of the world to look into the hearts of all mankind, everywhere. Her destiny was to find the basic reasons for the self-made tragedies of man in so beautiful a world.

The great purpose to which her life was dedicated compelled her to live a life of solitude of her own making without, however, withdrawing from the world of human activities.

At times she would leave some great city and seek solitude for meditation and "talking with God" in some remote place like the Sahara Desert, where she once lived for six months. There, she looked into the hearts of its unhappy peoples, especially its women who toiled hard for their husbands who sat lazily in the shade and performed no work at all. Such incidents as these nurtured her desire to bring balance into the world of mankind through the uplifting of women to equal status of men.

This brief sketch about Lao Russell's lifework and purpose should not close without a few words about her as an extraordinarily efficient woman in all of her activities. She is not only a perfectionist in all of her creations but a master of every activity she undertakes.

From early childhood she held larger scores in playing cribbage and other games with her father, and all through her life she excelled in the arts, games, and sports. She has won many trophies in dancing, tennis, table tennis, and other activities—sometimes even excelling the professionals in their particular fields. She is a superb dancer and I love to tell the story of her dancing with one of our students, who was a professional dancer, at a large gathering when they did an exhibition tango and waltz. Until that time no one knew of her talent in this field, because she had never mentioned her skill and great love for this form of art.

Whatever she sets her hand at doing she does with perfection, even though she has never attempted to master its technique before. Perhaps the most conspicuous example of the cosmic nature of her talents was when I was attempting to interpret her vision and concept of the Christ in the colossal statue of THE CHRIST OF THE BLUE RIDGE, which we erected in the gardens of our University at Swannanoa. At a crucial point during this work, I was not meeting the requirements which fulfilled her concept; so I spontaneously gave her a large handful of clay and said: *"You do it. You know that you can as well as I know that you can."*

Up to that very day she had never attempted sculpture although she had watched me work. She took the clay with full confidence and immediately modeled her own strongly masculine concept into the uplifted face of the Christ, and from that day on she did as much work upon it as I, and with equal masterliness. When others marveled because of it and asked her how she could possibly do such a marvelous thing, she merely replied, "Love did it through me. Love is the greatest power in the world. If you love deeply enough, and your desire is great enough, there is not anything within human possibilities that you cannot accomplish."

Her great beauty, her vibrant charm, and deep spiritual love for humanity, makes Lao Russell a personality one can never forget.

A short time before Walter Russell refolded, someone asked for a biography of Lao Russell from which they could quote. This introduction is part of that biography.

Part I

"Love is like unto the ascent of a high mountain peak. It comes ever nearer to you as you go ever nearer to it."

—From *Code of Ethics,*
by LAO RUSSELL

CHAPTER I

Love's Phantasy

"I love you with all my heart. I shall love you forever and ever." These are the words of lovers through all of the ages and, since love is all there is, who does not desire to hear them over and over again, day in and day out? One can *never* hear them often enough.

There is not a man, woman, or child, who does not desire and need love, for the purpose of life itself is to know and manifest love. Love is all there is in this great universe of man which he calls his world.

The great challenge of life is to find that love which is whole, steadfast and true. Man's senses, which he expresses through his physical emotions, can deceive him mightily. Only when he at last understands the difference between his senses and his Soul—or Mind-qualities—does he find that *lasting* romance which all men and women seek.

The great emotion that awakens in teen-agers is like a high voltage explosion. O, *how* tremendous it is—and how excitingly sensational. Your heart beats so fast you feel it will burst and that indescribable sex urge is overwhelming. You feel you *must* give your all. Only *all* of yourself will satisfy that explosive urge. But is it love—true love—which creates that tremendous urge or is it the desire to satisfy the senses?

Is this love's phantasy or is this true love? Even to question yourself at this glorious moment seems unthinkable . . . *and yet you must question it for the happiness of your whole life may rest upon this ecstatic moment's decision.*

In this twentieth century much emphasis has been placed upon *sex*—which is transitory—and too little upon *love*—which is eternal and is the highest goal of all mankind, whether he is aware of it or not.

We can only put into practice the things we *know* and the goal of this book is to help you to *know* the difference between LOVE and SEX so that you can reach the ultimate in happy matehood, which is the greatest joy and possession on earth.

When the world at long last knows the secret of happy matehood—which is *balanced matehood*— we shall have a happy, united, and balanced, world.

CHAPTER II

How to Attract Romance

DESIRE brings all things into being. Therefore, let your first desire be that you bring your ideal mate to you. Then do that which will attract him or her to you.

The great *secret* of *how* to attract romance is to *do only that which makes you loved*. And *what* is doing only that which makes you loved? The answer is very simple—*live love*.

Living love means putting others *first*. This will develop what some people describe as "empathy" which is an intuitive understanding of others' moods. However this characteristic is described, it is a combination of many things which comes from putting the feelings and desires of others first. Scientifically the reaction always equals the action; therefore, in first considering the other person, you are kindling his desire to regive to you that which YOU desire.

Everyone is seeking that certain someone with whom he can feel happy and *contented*. Contentment seems to express a deeper feeling than happiness. When we feel that we can be ourselves with someone, we feel *comfortable* and *contented* with him. Tensions do not build up between two people who have found the key to contentment. Consideration for each other is the key to romance and it is the natural expression of love.

There is an irresistible quality about a man or woman who puts love into every action. It is the little things about a person that attract you to him. And it is the little mannerisms that irritate and often break up a budding romance.

Humans are so geared that they take the big things in their stride but the little things can wreck an otherwise wonderful relationship.

No one can resist a truly loving person, and when one understands the art of living he has learned that *loving* everything he does not only brings joy to his own heart but he becomes as a magnet that draws others to him.

If we approach a chore with a happy attitude, we do it well, quietly, quickly, and smoothly. We feel good *inside*. If, on the other hand, we approach it whiningly, we do it badly, and slowly, and feel *irritated inside,* because we are really cross with *ourselves* for so acting. When we learn that only *we* suffer for our bad tempers and basic laziness, we learn to put love into all of our actions whether the task is a small or large one.

Our character traits are of the utmost importance for they shape not only what our face and body look like but they also shape our destiny. We are what we think, do, and say. *Therefore, to attract romance we*

6

must look, act, and express romance. We must *be* romance. This being so, let us first consider our faces, which is what first attracts us to each other.

THE QUALITIES WHICH ATTRACT

It has always been said that the eyes are the windows of the Soul. Eyes that express Soul-qualities —and these come under the heading of love, kindness, loyalty, and inner beauty—shine with a light that irresistibly draws you to them. It is not the color, shape, or size, that attracts but a quality of indefinable beauty. There is a light in the eyes of love that is beyond the senses of physical man. Everyone can have this irresistible quality if he lives love; and if he thinks love, he will *live* it. His every action will bespeak love for it will be smooth, flowing, and beautiful. A body is controlled by its thoughts and when these are rhythmical the body is, likewise, rhythmical in action. Your body develops in shape according to your thinking.

Clothes have a great effect on the way we feel. At heart we are all romanticists and a girl in a lovely gown feels far more romantic than she does in slacks. She knows that she looks alluring and more feminine.

What girl has not visioned herself floating down a church aisle in a long, beautiful wedding gown and sweeping veil? And how truly lovely and romantic are long chiffon evening gowns. There is rarely a woman whose heart does not thrill to the thought of dancing in a beautiful ballroom in the arms of her beloved. How proud a man is to hold such a beautifully gowned woman in his arms. That spells romance with a capital "R."

A woman's greatest asset is in *being* a woman. However beautiful a body is, it is far more fascinating when it is half hidden. Ask a truly masculine man about this and he will tell you that this is so. Of course I am speaking now only of day and evening clothes. Although the half hidden has its place in a lady's boudoir, also.

Love and romance are nurtured by trying to please each other. It is the little things that make the big difference in keeping a marriage alive and vibrant. Very few people are able to look their best in the early rush of the morning breakfast and getting to work. However, even if both are working, the evening mealtime offers a wonderful opportunity for romance. An inexpensive hostess gown, lounging pajamas, and dressing gown offer a more conducive atmosphere for sex appeal, respect, and admiration for each other. Candlelight and dinner music with the pleasant aroma of food can become a habit that pays handsome dividends from the bank of romance. These things make all of us feel more romantic after our work day. Changing into something "different" changes our thoughts and mood to one of love and romance.

When my beloved was alive I used to put on a long velvet or silk hostess gown in the evenings, for

8

these were the moments we always used for romancing each other. Our work never allowed time for socializing; so these moments were filled with the ecstasy of love's sharing.

He would wear a velvet or silk lounging coat, or robe, and we would talk "love talk" while having dinner. Sometimes we would have background music. All of our meals were prepared with love, for food cooked with love and eaten with love feeds all of one's hunger and makes for happy, healthy blood.

After dinner my beloved would play the organ for me before we started work again on a new book or other important work. These are the precious memories that now fill my Soul and give me inspiration to extend to youth the fruits of true love.

WHEN YOU CREATE BEAUTY, YOU EXPRESS ROMANCE

Create beauty in all you do, and beautiful things will always come into your life. We all desire beauty whether we are aware of this fact or not.

All of your thoughts are registered in your eyes, mouth, nose, and every contour of your face, as well as your body. You truly sculpture your character on your whole being. This is a tremendous thought, is it not? And one it is well to remember in your teen-age years when love and romance dominate your deepest thoughts and actions.

And what is expressing romance? Expressing romance is putting beauty into all that you do whether it be in the care you give your face and body, the clothes you wear, or the way you walk and talk.

My eyes always travel to a person's mouth. Here, I can read what life has wrought throughout the years. There are the lines of mirth, selflessness, kindness, tenderness, sensitivity or sorrow, or there are the lines of despair, selfishness, bitterness, jealousy, and envy. Nature delicately molds all of our character traits upon our mouths, and they cannot be erased or hidden as they can in the eyes. Sometimes the eyes can hide our feelings for a fleeting moment but we seldom *think* to control our mouths.

I heard a teacher say, when I was a child, *"Always go to sleep with a smile on your lips and you will wake up smiling."* She added, *"If you do not feel like smiling, push the corners of your mouth up with your thumb and finger. It will stay that way while you sleep."*

Not only does your face tell the story of your life and thinking, but so does your whole body. A posture expresses the life pattern of a mature person; how he has thought, how he has lived, whether he is governed by negative or positive thoughts, whether he is sensitive to the feelings of others, or whether he is callous and cruel. All these things one can see and sense in a person's presence.

Most powerful is that invisible "something" one is

attracted to. That "something" is one's character, and this time alone reveals *fully*.

THE BEAUTY WHICH COMES WITH MATURITY

My beloved husband, who was one of the world's greatest and most famous portrait painters, concentrated on children early in his career. In 1903–4 he was commissioned by the *Ladies' Home Journal* to choose and paint the twelve prettiest children in America.

However, in time, he desired to paint mature people who, he said, expressed so much more character through their living of life. He would say, *"A child's face is pretty; but life with its hills and valleys molds character on a face, and that is what I want to portray."*

I do not believe there has ever been an artist who has portrayed the Soul of a person in the eyes as my husband did in both his paintings and sculptures. Actually he was the first sculptor to put the iris in the eye and to so mold the eye that one can even tell whether the eyes are blue or brown.

Everything about you expresses YOU—the Soul of you. That is *why* it is important for you to express beauty of character, because a beautiful character *attracts* romance.

The most beautiful of women is the woman who has the charm that only a loving character can

11

express. And the most handsome of men is the one who has tenderness and sensitivity combined with the strength and power of pure masculinity.

A person who creates *beauty,* which is BALANCE, does not have the desire to create *ugliness,* which is UNBALANCE.

EVERYONE APPRECIATES ART

Many more people have an appreciation and desire for Beauty—which is ART—than is generally thought.

A young man said to me one day while visiting Swannanoa, *"You know, I do not really understand art but I really do like your husband's wonderful paintings and sculpture."*

I told him he liked them because they were true to nature. They are portraits of men and women looking as they are, not grossly distorted as some modern artists depict them. I said when you look at a tree my husband has painted, you *know* it is a tree—you do not have to make a guess as to *what* it is.

The young man and the other visitors agreed wholeheartedly with me when I said that many people thought they *should be able to understand* abstract paintings, which we describe as modern art, and said they were relieved to hear how I felt about many of them, and that now they did not feel as stupid and ignorant as they thought themselves to be.

Every item we use is first designed by an artist just

as every note of music we hear over the radio or television is first composed by an artist musician. The chair you sit in, the bed you sleep in, and the hammock you swing in were all designed by an artist. We are all prone to take these things that we use in our daily lives for granted, and there is not one of us who does not need a gentle reminder that everything we use was *first* the creation of an artist. Therefore it is a rare person who does not appreciate art in some form or another.

I remember this young man said he would never forget what I had told him and, from that moment on, I knew he would see with different eyes all things that surrounded him.

WE EARN LOVE AND ROMANCE

This past Sunday, I was talking to a fine young couple who said they had two daughters aged seven and twelve—although they looked like teen-agers themselves—and the man said, *"I have a wonderful wife. She has made me feel dependent upon her. When we go away, she packs my bag and does so many little things for me. I just could not get along without her."* To this I replied, *"And I am sure you do many little and big things for her. When she packs the bags, you undoubtedly drive the car."* To which he replied, *"You are right, I do drive the car and help her in any way that I can."* They were obviously a wonderfully balanced couple and you could tell they lived and worked for each other.

13

They were amazed and thrilled with all they found at Swannanoa, and I know I shall meet and talk with them many times as time goes by.

I am quite sure this young couple is bringing their children up to do little things for them and for each other, also. I recalled my own childhood, and how my mother had taught me to get my father's slippers and help him to change his shoes when he came in tired in the evening. This I was allowed to do as soon as I could toddle. I was walking before I was a year old, thanks to our precious Scotch collie dog.

My sisters and I were brought up to know it was a privilege to do things, and when each of us was allowed to wash the best china, we knew we had really arrived.

It never ceases to shock and surprise me when parents and children complain because of having to do necessary things like cooking, washing up, and cleaning, etc. I cannot help but feel that it is the early attitude of parents towards these things which make the children dislike doing them so much.

I have a nephew who stayed with me for several months when he was nine years old. I gave him all kinds of chores to do. Always I rewarded him with special privileges like taking him for a drive in the car or playing tennis. I taught him that we must *first give* so that we can be *regiven. Everything* must be earned.

This little boy has grown into a wonderful human being, and two years ago was given one of the highest awards ever given to a Boy Scout Master. He has been a Boy Scout since a very little boy. He told me that the many things I taught him as a child have helped him attain the high position he is in in his life and work today. He recently married a lovely girl. So he has "all this and heaven, too."

DISCIPLINE WITH LOVE

Those things we are taught as little children stay with us all of our lives. The older we get, the more likely we are to remember them. Discipline with love gives a child a sense of *being wanted. As children, we need discipline and guidance and, when we become adults, we have to discipline ourselves every day of our lives.*

Children, like adults, like to feel a sense of approbation, and they know that the one who gives them *loving* discipline wants to be proud of them. There is not a thing that hurts children more than when they hear their mother unduly praising other children and ignoring them. Instead of making children want to excel, it often puts them in reverse and they do the "wrong" thing, which ultimately makes them hate themselves. This is usually the beginning of what we call "juvenile delinquency."

Humans, both children and adults, are deeply sensitive and critical of *themselves,* and this will express itself in either an "I don't care" attitude or an overbearing, superiority attitude.

The early years are of extreme importance and

children respond to beauty and love when they know you *care* what happens to them without, of course, "smothering" them.

CHARACTER BUILDING IN EARLY YOUTH

My husband wrote a beautiful children's book entitled, *The Bending of the Twig*. This book, as its name implies, conveys the importance of character building in children from an early age. Many thinking parents are distressed that too little emphasis is placed upon character building today and that the need for this influence in books, radio, television, and other media of education and entertainment, must be filled.

I am deeply grateful for the love and discipline my own mother and father gave me. My mother was so kind and gentle, one just could not be naughty. And my father was a great disciplinarian. I remember one day saying "O.K." at the luncheon table. I did not realize my father was so averse to slang, but the impression he made upon me was so deep regarding the use of slang words that even to this day I have a sense of guilt if I use them.

My father was one of the most ethical and honest men I have ever known. He would not make a debt of even one penny. He taught us never to buy anything that we could not pay for first. As a consequence, my sisters and I never made a debt, and this has always given us a wonderful sense of freedom.

My parents truly loved us. We spent wonderful

evenings doing things together. Every evening, my father, who was fifty-four when I was born, would play games with me—games that developed my brain and made me think. And then weekends, we would all go for long walks in the country. My parents loved nature and wildlife. Father was an expert horseman, ice skater, and dancer. Mother was the poet and musician, and father loved singing while she played. He was also a deep student of human nature and loved reading.

I am, also, deeply grateful to a beloved elder sister who was left my guardian when my parents died when I was twelve years old. She had the highest principles and ideals, and we had a wonderful sharing of all things that were beautiful.

All of the character traits of parents, and those close to us in our early years, greatly affect our thinking, and they either give us a head start in life or handicap us. Learning early what is *right* gives a child a sense of security which will hold him in good stead for the rest of his life.

What a child *most* needs is to know that someone truly *cares* what happens to him. This is what *all* people need—young or old.

Character building projects all over this country, and throughout the world, would bring into being a greater Age of Character. So very many could aid in the organization of the worldwide International Age of Character Clubs described at the end of this book. The Consciousness of the world would be lifted by each and every individual who so desired and

17

worked with any movement that had character building as its basic purpose.

LIVE LOVE

How many girls and boys there are who feel romance is passing them by! It should not be so—and will not be so—if they truly learn to live love, for *the inviolate Law of Life is that life gives to us in equal measure that which we give to it.*

If this thought of living love is new to you, let me explain it a little more explicitly. To live love means having no thought of what *you* are going to *get* from whatever you may do—only of what *you* can *give.*

For instance, let us suppose tomorrow is your mother's birthday—or it is Father's Day—and you want to make her or him happy. The gift that you give which is thoughtlessly purchased—however beautiful or expensive it may be—will not give the joy to the receiver that a small gift will which has taken time and thought to make or procure. The time given to prepare a little party for a mother or father is a heartwarming experience for any parent. And the same thing goes for a friend.

The sweetheart who thinks of little surprises for the loved one shows that his or her thoughts are with the beloved. It does not have to be a big gift to please. It is *not* that we want money spent on us; it is just that we all like knowing we are thought of, *constantly.*

I cherish the memory of my mother's father, whom I never knew, because mother told me that grandfather never came home from a trip—and he made many—that he did not bring grandmother some little gift, even if it was but a small bunch of flowers. The last thing he brought her, which was a few days before she died very suddenly, was a beautiful hand-stitched text, *"Love Is Strong As Death."*

Knowing my grandparents shared such a beautiful love has meant so much to me all of my life. It will keep them alive in my heart forever.

THE FALLACY OF THE "AGE" QUESTION

Today's emphasis on age has become an obsession in the western world. In the East age is revered, but in the West we have reached the point of thinking that youth must always be stressed as a goal to reach and keep. This emphasis on age has influenced teen-age thinking. Many girls of eighteen, who have never had a regular "date," feel they are passé. A girl or boy of eighteen is just beginning to *really* think about life, and far from being "left on the shelf," can be more exciting and entertaining to the opposite sex than a younger person.

It has become a habit for people to ask immediately upon hearing about, or meeting someone, "How old is she?"—"How old is he?" This question is unimportant because it is nonessential. Some people are far more mentally unfolded at twenty than others at forty. *Age is important only from the standpoint of knowledge.*

As far as *looking* young is concerned, this is far

19

more dependent on mental attitude than on chronological age. Emphasis should be placed on developing the Mind and then people would feel, act and *be* "young in heart."

Thinking about looking old develops "worry" lines and brings a worried look into the eyes. This will create an illusion of age however young the person. On the other hand, the one who is natural and mentally alert, with a joyful attitude, creates an illusion of youth whatever his age.

When two people love each other, age is no problem whatever the age difference may be. We become unaware of age when there is a meeting of minds. Mind is eternal and, therefore, ageless. When it comes to romance, every man and woman feels like a teen-ager *inside*. We are never too old or too young to fall in love.

Understanding what Mind is brings a realization that Mind controls matter (body) and this is why people with active, vibrant mentalities always attract to themselves people of *all* ages.

Your thinking gives birth to all that attracts or detracts. Therefore, start thinking through your Mind, which means to think *inwardly,* and not through your *senses* which means *outwardly*.

We would have far more lasting romances if people found *mental* companionship with each other. Body attraction *alone* will never keep romance alive. The frustration of thinking you are too young—or too old—will no longer haunt you as you realize that it is *not* your *body* which really attracts. It is your Soul qualities which attract because your Soul *is* love.

THE GREAT IMPORTANCE OF RESPECT

Since it is the Soul-qualities which we cannot see but can *know* that really attract, these are the qualities to strive for. Therefore, the true meaning of romance is *respect*.

The reason these qualities are of the *greatest* importance is that, unless we have a deep respect for the object of our affections, our romance will not be a *lasting* one. *It will end in disillusion and disappointment.*

When our hearts long for romance, we all too often settle for *any* person rather than wait for *the* person.

A conversation with a disillusioned man in his late thirties revealed the sad story of settling for less than the ideal. He told me how he was reared on a farm and went to college in a big city. He was then twenty-one and very lonely in a new strange world and, when he met a girl whom he was physically attracted to, he married her. After a few years, the marriage ended in divorce. Then he met another girl to whom he was again physically attracted. They went to parties together, drank cocktails together, went to movies together, and did all the other physical and socializing things men and women do together, never really spending time just discovering

21

each other's Mind-thinking. They eventually married, and he said that just one hour after they were married he *knew* he had made a mistake, adding he lived with his "mistake" for seven and a half years.

There are many people who live with this same kind of mistake for years and years—sometimes a whole lifetime. Children come along, economic conditions, religious ties, fear of what others will say, and various other reasons keep people *tied* to each other for years. But are they happy? Do they have a *true* marriage in the sight of God? Is it *fair* to the children?

All these miseries could be *avoided* if only idealism for a true and balanced mate, for whom one has a deep respect, had been the motivating desire in the beginning. *It is far, far better to be lonely alone than to be lonely with someone.*

THOSE IMPORTANT TWENTY-THREE HOURS

After talking to me, the man with the two broken marriages mentioned above said, *"I would not have married either time if I had heard what you said regarding the twenty-three hours of companionship."* I had told him that one should only marry someone with whom he could spend twenty-three hours of good solid companionship. If he could not do this he should run fast. *When* we can spend twenty-three hours of companionship—talking or just sharing moments of golden silence—the other hour of physical interchange in sex relations and dining together will be ecstatic. Otherwise physical intercourse loses its stimulating attraction, and even dining together becomes a bore.

The great challenge is to make yourself into the kind of person who will attract that special one that your heart and Soul desires. You can never have a true and lasting romance until *you are romance,* and you can *be* romance by living love, which means expressing the qualities of love.

THE MOMENTS WE CHERISH

The moments we cherish as we go through life are the moments of joy we have shared. Your capacity of *knowing* joy *equals* your capacity of *giving* joy.

When you know deep joy, you reflect that joy to your companion. *This is how we attract romance.* That deep joy within you is what you recognize in that other one. It is that "something" everyone is forever seeking. Once you find it, *tend it and cherish it*—for it is LOVE.

The *power* of love is the *greatest* power on earth. That power is yours when you do all things *with* love.

CHAPTER III

Victory over Guilt
and Frustrations

Guilt is a self-inflicted wound. It takes loving understanding to heal it. Frustration and hatred follow the same pattern.

Self-forgiveness of our weaknesses is as important as our forgiveness of others' weaknesses.

Forgiveness has the connotation of *condescension*. We should always strive to *understand* what was the motivating thought behind our own or our fellow man's actions. Then, rather than say, "I forgive you," say, "I understand." When we truly understand *what* motivates our every thought, we learn to control our actions.

MANY PROBLEMS CREATED BY MISUNDERSTANDINGS

Most of our problems and heartaches are created by a misunderstanding of each other. We forget that each one of us has his or her own way of seeing things and of expressing thoughts. We hurt each other so often when it is the last thing we want to do. And the one we love the most of all, we hurt the most of all.

24

This is because we are closest to the one we love, and in the intimacy of our close relationship we sometimes do not stop to think long enough to censure what we say.

Lovers all through the ages have hurt each other. How often we hear or read of "a lovers' quarrel" and the sweetness of "making up."

As we grow more mature in thought, we learn to stop and think a little before expressing irritation. However, life in this twentieth century is full of tensions, and that is why there is a greater need for deep understanding. Everyone desires to be happy, and in loving understanding of each other lies the hope of greater happiness for every individual and for all the world.

OVERCOMING SELF-CONDEMNATION

Many a life that has known the shadow of guilt has been ruined because of self-condemnation which has led to frustration and a great fear of life itself.

There has never been a person on this earth who has not done "something" he wishes he had not done. It is helpful—and healing—to remember this when you feel alone, cast out from society and utterly miserable.

Sex can be the most uplifting and inspiring experience, or it can make one feel degraded and unclean. I remember my husband telling me the story about a man who had been a great idealist, but who had been caught up in sex perversion with a group through his work. He was a script writer. It made him feel so degraded and unclean that he did not want to live. His father asked my husband to go many miles to talk to him because he feared that he would take his own life. However, this man could not surmount his feelings of self-disgust, and eventually he did commit suicide.

Had he been able to overcome his self-condemnation, he would have learned that he could build a new life for himself and, *because* of his own overcoming, be able to help others to see why living without compromise reaps the rich reward of inner peace.

A sense of guilt can be overcome by doing what we know to be right. Scientifically, we cannot carry a guilt throughout our lives. Everything that happens is voided as it happens. The record is ever within our memory record but, unless we *repeat* that which gave us a sense of guilt, it cannot continue to be a guilt. *Therefore, see every incident in your life for what it is—an experience which taught you something.*

Whatever you have said or done that makes you unhappy, or gives you a feeling of guilt or failure, know it was a *good* experience for it made you *think.*

When you fully realize *what your purpose on earth is,* you will realize that the incidents in your life are of *secondary* importance, and that what you gain in understanding from them is of *primary* importance. You will then have learned one of *the*

26

most important lessons of life. You will go forward free in thought and action.

The *most* important lesson to learn from any incident that caused you the agony of mental torture is not to allow the *same kind of incident to occur again. You* gave birth to your agonies by your thoughts and actions, and only *you* can repeat that experience. You may have other experiences which cause you pain, and you may have to overcome other weaknesses in your character, but with each overcoming you become a stronger character.

Overcoming a weakness in your character gives you greater understanding and compassion for the weaknesses you find in others. This loving understanding will draw others to you, and the chain reaction leads to greater love awakening in all men's hearts for each other.

The greatest Teacher of Love ever to be on earth told the woman at the well to *"Go and sin no more."* He knew that as soon as she ceased to do that which was called "sin," she would forgive herself. Only *you* can overcome your so-called faults by not expressing them again.

THE DANGER OF GOSSIP

One of the most destructive traits in the human character is gossip. It is a complete violation of the Law of Love, and that is *why* it is so destructive.

Gossip is not based on constructive things and ideas, but on nonessential incidents of passing sensational interest. The great tragedy, however, is the permanent damage to the gossiper's personality, and the irrevocable harm to other sensitive souls.

I recall the incident of a young girl who had been taken home by the father of her girl friend after a dance. A neighbor had seen her get out of the car at one o'clock in the morning, and the man had taken her to her door. The neighbor drew her warped conclusions and started a story that this young girl was having "an affair" with Mr. So and So.

The girl denied the story at first and told what really happened. However, once the story was circulated, it grew out of all proportions. This ugly untruth so preyed on this young girl's mind that she finally committed suicide.

This story is but one example of countless stories of tragedies that would never happen if people were kindly, loving, and understanding.

Ironically, a gossiper does not realize that he is reflecting his own desires and faults to the one he condemns. It is less "painful" to his ego to condemn the other person than admit his own weaknesses. People who gossip are those who *need* love and understanding, for it is a deep-rooted sense of insecurity, frustration, and inferiority that causes them to gossip. People *think* that in tearing others down they are building themselves up whereas, in reality, they are parading their own deficiencies.

Because of inner dissatisfaction with ourselves, there is a tendency within most of us to give credit with faint praise. For instance, a person will say, *"She is a lovely woman but . . ."* or, *"He is a brilliant man but . . ."* It is a rare person who feels secure enough within himself to give praise without reservation.

There is an odd characteristic in all of us because, although we inwardly resent hearing another criticized, we still savor a little gossip about their misfortunes. It is only by constant and thoughtful vigilance that we can control and overcome this universal trait.

OUR GREATEST CHALLENGE

How many wonderful teen-agers have died—committed suicide even—because of a deep sense of guilt and frustration!

That is *why* it is important for young people—and older ones, also—to realize fully that a frustrating experience is *not* the end of life and happiness for them. From an unhappy experience, they can build a new way of life that will lead to greater happiness. Life *never* stands still, and we *grow* with the hardest and most heartbreaking experiences. Life is like a school—and we are *all* students of Life.

We are never too young to sense the difference between right and wrong. When that Inner Voice whispers to us, and we heed it, we can save ourselves untold agonies. *The choice is always ours.*

Our *greatest* challenge in life is the battle between the Soul and the senses. *No one escapes that battle.*

29

Our greatest victory is when Soul wins. This victory shines from our eyes and brings us ever closer to our goal of True Love.

COMPROMISE DELAYS FULFILLMENT

I remember, one Sunday, a boy and girl came to visit our Shrine of Beauty at Swannanoa. The hostess came to me and said there was a young girl with her date, in the gold music room, who she felt was very unhappy and would I go and talk to her. I knew intuitively what her problem was even before I saw her. She was with a boy whom she did not really love but she felt she *must* have a date or be a failure; so here she was keeping company with a boy who obviously bored her because they were too unlike to be truly companionable. I said to her, *"Why are you here with this boy whom you do not really like?"* She said, *"How do you know I do not care for him?"* I told her that I was sixteen once and had felt that I had to have a boy friend—come what may. I went on to tell her that some day she would realize—as we all do—that compromising *never* brings our heart's desire to us. *It keeps it away just so long as we compromise.* I told her to stop compromising and that the one her heart truly desired would *come* to her. I said it may be six months or even a year but it *would* happen. She said that her mother had told her the same thing but she would not listen to her.

We can be told a truth a thousand times and it does not strike a responsive chord, but the thou-

30

sandth and one time it is crystal clear. This time the truth about compromise did make sense to that young girl.

About eight months later, the hostess came and said there was a young couple who was terribly eager to see me. It was that same young girl, eyes shining and bright with love, with her handsome young prince. They had become engaged that very day, and she wanted to share her joy with me. She told me how she had waited six long months for the *right* boy to come into her life, but now it was all well worth waiting for.

Sometimes we have to wait much, much longer than a few months for our true love to come to us, but however long the wait may be when he or she does meet us on our horizon, time dissolves into nothingness.

That deep desire within every heart for a beloved mate has caused many young people to compromise with their ideals. Only knowledge of *why* compromise delays the fulfillment of our dreams will make us stop and consider our actions. It is not easy when your body cries out for the touch that thrills. The climb to our mountain-top becomes ever more challenging with every step upward, but that view from the topmost peak is too deep for words—it truly is heaven.

There is so much to tell of compromise and *how* it delays us in the fulfillment of our desires. To write fully of the long detours that compromise brings to us through life is scientifically explained in our other books and teachings. Now it is all important that you can better understand yourself in regard to romance and the sex urge which motivates your thinking and actions, and guides you to your perfect love or to the misery which is born of compromise.

Let us again consider that sense of guilt which comes when sex is indulged in without love and marriage. *This self-condemnation comes from the frustrating lack of complete fulfillment.* Everyone desires complete fulfillment. It is not just a sex fulfillment; it is a fulfillment of *all* of one's self. It is the deep desire for oneness with the other half of one's self.

When you have sex without love, you know deep within yourself that this is *not* what you really want; and, when the passions have been spent, you begin thinking through your Mind-Self instead of through the superficial stream of your senses. You *know* that you desire *mental-sharing* as well as *body-sharing*. You may not think of sex intercourse in these terms, but that is what it really is. You *know* that when it is *not* love, all you satisfied was your *body*. You feel soiled and have a deep sense of guilt and frustration because you know you want something more—something much *deeper* than just body sharing. You also know deep within that this kind of sex—or body sharing—cannot last and did not even satisfy your *body* desires fully. You may not know *why*, but you do know that you are filled with a deep sense of frustration instead of the exaltation you had dreamed about. *You are so frustrated, you feel you want to die.* A girl has a sense of guilt at such times, and a boy a sense of being trapped and obligated. It is because both want love—true balanced mated love.

When two people know sex with love, it is a beautiful uplifting experience that inspires both with beauty. The true wonder, beauty, romance, and ecstasy of sex is not known when it has to be a hurried "stolen thrill."

When man understands that the scientific principle of *all* Creation is the *holy law of mating,* which we call SEX, and that nothing can be given form without it, he will be filled with reverence for *himself* and desire beauty of Creation to be expressed through him and his balanced spiritual, mental and physical mate. Sex intercourse with one's spiritual, mental, and physical mate is the ultimate in ecstasy, and for one brief moment one melts into oneness with the universal heart-beat and becomes unaware of body consciousness. This ecstasy is only known in balanced matehood and, like all things else in life, *must be earned* through a period of adherence to Natural Law in all of one's interchangings. Compromising with one's ideals for a momentary thrill can *never* bring the perfection of true love. The tragedy is for those who do not know this inviolate law of the universe which is *Rhythmic Balanced Interchange.*

33

Beautiful sex is like beautiful music—the melody lingers on *forever*.

FROM ALL THAT IS UNLOVELY TURN THINE EYES

When I was quite young, I discovered a little book entitled, *Thoughts Are Things*. It was written by Prentice Mulford. It made a great impression upon me. I remember he said that looking at or reading murder stories attracted such things to you. I would never look at, listen to, or read such stories afterwards. I never did enjoy murder stories, and intuitively knew we brought into our lives that which we envisioned. I was never happier than when writing or reading fairy stories. This I did from a very early age.

Thoughts truly are things, for this is a thought-wave universe, and we are all giant transmitting and receiving stations.

TELEVISION—ESCAPE FROM REALITY

Watching television has largely become an escape mechanism from reality. Personal frustrations are the main reason for this escapism. Millions have become slaves to television instead of truly enjoying it. It *is* a great source of enjoyment for those who use it wisely; but when it is a day-long escape from reality, it really builds up tensions and cancels out its true purpose, which is to entertain and inspire.

Thinking people realize it has an hypnotic appeal

and, instead of uniting friends and families, it has separated many of them. People will tell you that each member of their family has a favorite program, and woe betide any other member of the family who even speaks to that one who is watching his or her favorite program. How can such a family have fun doing the little intimate things together that *make* a family.

We hear so often today that people do not visit with each other anymore. I am quite sure that one reason for this is that when friends go to visit, and the television is going full blast, they do not want to stay and scream to make themselves heard over the noise and racket of the television.

This wonderful instrument that could be such a joy has become a pest in many instances. It has become one of the major causes of creating moronic young people instead of bright, intelligent children who know the joy and satisfaction of creating.

If we had more programs to educate and inspire, that would be *constructive*. However, murder stories are *destructive*.

A TEMPORARY SEDATIVE

Many women have their televisions going all day and listen to the woeful stories of intrigue and unrequited love, and other negative incidents in unbalanced lives. One woman told me recently that *"listening to the awful things that happened in other people's lives had made me think that my own life was not so bad after all."* She was not happy and satisfied with her life, and actually said she did not make a move to try to change it because of the influence that the television stories had upon her. To such people television is a temporary sedative.

This same woman's life was abruptly changed through a set of circumstances, beyond her control, which forced her out into the world. Today she is happier than ever before in her life. She is now helping others to understand the basic cause of *their* problems. Because she had lived a life of frustration, she can help others more effectually than she otherwise might have been able to do. Suffering gives us greater compassion for others, because we understand the underlying *cause* of the mental distortions which give birth to almost all of our individual sufferings.

We are all so apt to think that the dreadful things just happen to us, and that no one ever had to overcome such awful experiences. This is not so. Everyone goes through "dreadful" and "awful" experiences at one time or another. When the nightmare experience is over, it is like the sunshine appearing after a terrible storm. The heavens are blotted out with heavy clouds, thunder vibrates through the heavens shaking the earth in tumultuous claps of thunder, and it seems the very earth itself will be swallowed up in the fury of the storm. Then the golden sun comes peeping through, and the storm clouds disappear. Day melts into evening and the heavens are heavy with twinkling stars. A new moon shines its silver promise of a night of love and romance. All in twenty-four hours this change can come into being. And so it is with life itself when we know love in our hearts.

As so often happens when I am writing a News-letter or Christmas Message to our students, a letter comes from a student of our Home Study Course or books that expresses so beautifully the subject I am currently writing about. The following letter just arrived from a student who has hitched her wagon to a star and is riding high to the goal of her mountain-top. I feel inspired to share it with YOU:

Dear Lao Russell:

I have been wanting to write you for some time . . . This Unit 9 just made me "tingle" all over. I find myself exulting, "How wonderful! How beautiful! How perfectly magnificent!"

One will, indeed, continue to go over and over the lessons through the years. One can almost spot one's strengths and weaknesses as the different paragraphs take hold of one at different times. Some I read say, "Yes, THIS I have always been certain of." Others make me exclaim, "This is where I've made my mistakes."

The biggest difficulty of all, to me, is to read the newspapers, particularly as a court reporter being aware of all the poor struggling humanity, and know what to say or do. I have long ago found that I cannot help people beyond their desire to be helped

37

in their understanding of the thing you are trying to say.
The science part of your course—do the great re-search laboratories have it? The space age groups? I hope some day to meet you in person! I am truly thrilling to the great truths you set forth. I, too, as a youngster was one to seek to be alone—much—and still am, but was "timid"; I find myself "expanding" tremendously to find so many things one has felt, to be so wonderfully explained, and one's mind starts soaring, soaring, soaring.

Thank you . . . V. W.

How my heart sang as I read the letter this morning. How I shared this wonderful Soul's ecstasy, and how I long for *all* people to become aware of their inner selves. Some day there will be millions of awakened souls instead of the few who now hold the world's balance. When that day dawns, when fear leaves man and love enters, the age of slaughter of man by man will end and the age of character will begin.

THE GREAT OPPORTUNITY OF TV AND RADIO

Many parents wish their children would not stay "glued" to their sets for hours. The best way to stop this is by replacing television with something that they will enjoy *doing*.

Many people tell me they have discontinued their television viewing because they do not wish their children to waste time listening and looking at the type of programs given. I am sure they *would* enjoy some of the programs but they know that, once they turn their sets on, the children never want to turn them off, and then they see programs which are a bad influence.

Recently, two families visiting Swannanoa told me that they did not have a TV in their homes because they wanted their children to learn to *do* things themselves. They said that most of the programs were quite unsuitable for children and taught them nothing.

After hearing one of my talks to a group of visitors, a doctor told me that he always wished he could wake people up in his community to do something about the present decadent trend. He made a suggestion that fitted right in with the feelings that the previous two families had expressed regarding the *opportunity* of TV and radio stations. He said, *"If only they would have SPOTS which would stimulate the desire of people to be better people, I believe that would help us all tremendously. Continual spots to develop character fits in with all you said today."*

The very same morning, a young girl interested in helping young people asked me if I would talk to the young members of her church who, she said, *"lacked drive and seemed to have no desire to do anything."*

Surely the doctor's suggestion for TV and radio

spots is an excellent one, and these short reminders would *stimulate* a desire to listen to constructive radio and television programs.

All young people like to *do* things; and to have programs that teach them *how* to create and build things would open many *new* markets for industry.

Instead of boys having toy trucks, aeroplanes, boats, etc., given to them ready made, these could be sold in sections, and they could have television programs showing them *how* to assemble them.

And for girls, there are countless ideas which could be used from making dolls' clothes to cookery lessons.

Boys and girls *like* doing these important *everyday* things if they are so encouraged. I reiterate it is wrong to put the stamp of "chore" on domestic necessities. Viewing all domestic "chores" from a standpoint of creating BEAUTY is far more important. An untidy, dusty room is like seeing a tousled, unshaven man, or a woman with an unclean face and untidy hair. Such things certainly do not attract romance, and will certainly not *hold* it.

Lots of people, of all ages, love to create in ceramics, and this could become a big business for both the TV people and the suppliers of the materials.

Constructive, creative programs would be good for people in every way. They would aid in uniting families, stimulating friendships, and certainly in creating new and better businesses.

This does not in any way belittle the fact that television and radio are not *great* contributions to humanity. Their value is inestimable to shut-ins, people left alone in the world, and those who spend constructive lives in their businesses and share happy family life. For these people, such mediums are wonderful "company" and relaxation. There are plenty of fine programs for intelligent viewers and listeners. The above comments are directed to those who have not "found" themselves, and use TV and radio as they would and *do* use alcohol, drugs, and smoking, etc.

It is always a matter of *balance*.

People who do not *think* for themselves *demand* the type of program which takes them into a world of make-believe to offset the frustration of *purposeless* lives. To a large extent the industry gives the public the type of entertainment it demands. It is not in business for its health, but to make money, and if the type of show the public demands is what makes money, it will produce that type of show. So the fault, therefore, lies not so much with those who produce the programs as with those who demand them.

My husband and I attended movies only three times over a period of fifteen years. Therefore, I am not in a position to comment on present day movies. We were always so busy creating that we did not have the desire to see others portraying life. We were busy living out the drama of our own lives.

When you are deeply in love with each other, which means you are deeply in love with life, you do not feel such a need for outside entertainment. Not that we did not enjoy a fine movie, a fine TV show or good radio—we did, *greatly*. We always planned to see good shows and do more things *outside* together when we had finished writing all of our books. Now that I am alone, I love to listen to beautiful music coming over the radio when I go to bed, and there are many fine programs on both TV and radio to keep one informed of current events. Loneliness can truly be a thing of the past for anyone who is discerning enough to listen to good programs.

I understand, however, that many movies have reached an all-time low in entertainment value. People have expressed great disgust to me regarding the sordidness of sex movies.

Powerful dramas and beautiful musicals would undoubtedly fill movie houses again. Young and old like to be uplifted, for all can have a surfeit of sordid sex. This, also, is no doubt due to public demand. So if you teen-agers will begin demanding movies that lift the Consciousness, which will create the desire in you to *do* things that satisfy your *inner* selves rather than *over*-stimulate your *outer* senses, I am sure producers will oblige.

Popular demand for anything springs from popular DESIRE. It is well for all of us to remember that it is easier for a person to be pulled down to a sensed-level than to climb to spiritual heights. But, as I have stated before—and as we all know—the most beautiful and exhilarating view is from the *top*. Make up *your* mind to reach for the stars, and some day you will be the bright star in someone's life.

The mediums of television and radio have a tremendous opportunity today to bring into being a new age of character which truly would increase trade since, as most people now realize, we are living in a period where fear has brought lethargy to many individuals who need the stimulus that creativity brings.

WHAT IS *YOUR SECRET DESIRE* TO CREATE

There are many people, of all ages, who have a secret desire to create something. They get excellent *ideas,* but know not how to proceed with them. There is a creative and inventive streak in many people and, if this is fostered, it can become very productive. When we do create or invent some little thing, we get a great feeling of inner satisfaction.

This brings to my mind a little story you might enjoy. King Albert of Belgium had my beloved husband's famous painting, THE MIGHT OF AGES, on exhibition in his country for six months. At the time, this picture had been chosen by the plenipotentiaries of the King of Italy to represent American art at the Turin International Exposition of Art, which was to be held in 1900, in commemoration of the Twentieth Century. Many European countries asked for permission to have this magnificent painting on exhibition in their countries, Belgium being one of them.

King Albert greatly admired this wonderful picture and, when he visited the United States, he wanted to meet the artist who had painted it. He visited my husband in his studio in New York. The visit was to be brief. However, at the time of his visit, my husband was spending odd moments carving a mantel. The King was so excited to discover that Walter Russell was a wood-carver, also, that he confided to him that he had always had a *secret desire* to do wood-carving. He spent the whole morning carving one of the posts of a mantel we now have on exhibition at Swannanoa. I would perhaps have never known about this but, when I was having a stand made upon which to erect it, while staining and polishing it, I noticed one post was not quite as good as the others; and I said to my husband, *"You slipped up on this post, darling. It is not as good as the others."* I remember he laughed when he replied, *"I'll tell you something, I did not carve that post; King Albert of Belgium carved it."* Then he told me how the King had always wanted to do wood-carving, and how he was supposed to visit with two other people in New York that day, but never got beyond my husband's studio because of spending so many hours whittling away on the mantel.

It was by utilizing every moment constructively that my husband accomplished so much. He never wasted a moment in his long life. He always had that little boy quality of wanting to *do* something. As soon as we had finished doing anything, he would say, *"And now what shall we do?"*

BOYS' AND GIRLS' CLUBS

Just before writing about the part TV and radio could play in inspiring young people to create, I was talking to a mother with two lovely teen-age daughters. I was telling them a little about the contents of this book, and how much I hoped that it would help teen-agers—and *all* ages—to a happier way of life.

I asked the girls if they would like to have a club started in their town where they could learn arts and crafts, hold dances and have community singing, as well as have indoor and outdoor games like tennis, swimming, etc., and meet young men who would also like to take part in these activities. I wish you could have seen their eyes light up. They said they would *love* such a club in their town. I told them I had plans for these clubs, and would be giving details about them in this book.

There has been a great need for boys' and girls' clubs where they are taught to *do* things. Not clubs with dues so high that the average girl and boy cannot join, but clubs within the reach of all. These clubs, which would be building *character,* would be a far better investment than all the millions spent to curb delinquency. Creating beauty together, and taking part in competitive games, gives birth to a spirit of camaraderie and gets rid of that youthful energy *constructively*.

Sex has become something to indulge in for want of a better thing to do. The type of movies shown today has not helped in this regard, and neither has television. The trouble stems from a combination of many things. Idealism should first start in the home, be carried through in schools, and added to through public media such as newspapers, magazines, movies, radio, and television. *All media would be far more successful in every way with Idealism and Truth as their basis*. These changes can become a reality if people will exert the needed effort behind the *right* movements. Today the need for Idealism and Truth is a very real need which *must* be met. Everyone can do his or her part to fill this need.

TO CREATE IS TO LIVE

It is when we are doing creative things like painting, sculpturing, dancing, singing, dramatic acting, or taking part in activities such as tennis, basketball, football, skating, swimming, or any other challenging games, that we know the exhilaration of accomplishment.

The inner satisfaction of accomplishment is so necessary to us because, when we have that satisfaction, we know such a deep sense of joyousness that our desire to do even more is quickened.

When we feel that sense of achievement, we are happy inside. Always watching others, or listening to them, does not give us the satisfaction of actual *personal* accomplishment.

It is when we feel "empty" that we are prone to seek bodily sensations such as excessive drinking or smoking, which all too often lead to over-stimulation of purely sexual appetites.

Balance is the keynote to all and everything. *Excessive drinking, smoking, narcotics, and sex, can only lead to greater frustration, for they are all due to unbalanced desires.*

ALCOHOLISM, NARCOTICS AND SEX EXCESSES

The alcoholic has *become* an alcoholic because he is not *satisfied* with himself. He feels he wants to go beyond his senses to the ecstasy of weightlessness of body, to a dream-world of power which, in truth, is a state of forgetfulness of body-sensing, and yet a phantasy of power projection. It brings a false sense of command of pressing obligations, and events that seem to be holding him to a never ending tread-mill.

Alcoholics, or slaves to any body-addiction, can be rehabilitated as soon as they recognize and admit their weakness. A permanent change can only be effected by their own effort.

A right thinking person cannot tolerate a person who is intoxicated with alcohol, or any form of narcotic excesses. These excesses are the result of escape from reality.

47

Alcoholism grows out of boredom and self-pity, and everyone can overcome these destructive traits by doing things *for* other people. A shortcut to rehabilitate one's self from any weakness is to start helping someone else to help himself. You will be so busy that you will not have time for self-pity, which can lead to frustration, fear and ultimately self-hate. This *self*-hate spreads like a cancer to *world*-hate and the eventual fall of civilization.

The day after my beloved was buried, I went into my office early in the morning, and worked until the wee hours of the following morning. In writing letters to help others, I helped myself. I could have sat and cried all day. I longed for my sweetheart's pulsing presence beside me. Knowing we were as close in Mind as we ever were did not take that yearning away for the physical smile and handclasp. Nothing ever does.

The best cure for alcoholism, or any excessive and unbalanced condition in our lives, is *selflessness.* Give this explanation to someone who needs it. Remember that the alcoholic, the excessive smoker, the drug addict, or the sex maniac, is not *satisfied* with himself, and is trying to lose himself in excesses to *find* himself. Help him to know how really wonderful he is when he is true to his higher self. This he can unfold *within* himself through Mind-awareness. Later you will read *How* Mind-awareness slowly unfolds within you and transforms your thinking from physical-sensing to Mind-knowing, wherein lies your greatest power.

SELFLESSNESS is beautifully expressed by many members of Alcoholics Anonymous. These selfless members will get out of bed in the middle of the night, and go to the aid of a "fallen" brother or sister, if necessary, to give that one the moral courage to desist from taking another drink. They understand the plight of their "brothers" and "sisters," for they have overcome this particular weakness themselves. Loving understanding is surely one of our greatest assets. *Understanding is love in action.*

NATURE THRILLS AND HEALS

If your workaday life makes it impossible to take part in any creative or sports activity for the time being, just take walks together. This costs nothing, and is the best exercise you can have. As you walk along together, you can share your innermost thoughts and dreams with each other—and what could be greater fun?

Who has not longed for that special "someone" with whom to share a walk in the woods? Sharing the beauty of Nature's wonderland—looking at blue skies and billowing clouds—discovering a spider's web studded with drops of rain shimmering in the sunlight like a million jewels on a spun silk cloth.

Nature is a *balancing* antidote for our world grown so apathetic with material wealth. Diamonds

49

do not make you catch your breath the way Nature's fairyland of sparkling icicles can in a forest after a frost. One of *the* most beautiful experiences in my life happened one day when I was walking through the woods with my dog, and every little twig of every tree was glistening in the sunshine so that all the little "whiskers" were as though carved in ice. I embraced a tree and through my tears of joy said to my little Scotty, *"This is the most wonderful day of my life."* I shall share that moment with that little dog's soul through eternity, for the beauty of the woods and the love in her eyes are as real to me today, fifteen years later, as at that moment.

When relating the above experience to my beloved husband, we relived that moment together for he, being an artist and poet, shared my deep joy of Nature. His deep love and appreciation of Nature is revealed in his beautiful book entitled *The Book of Early Whisperings*. He was inspired to write this because of his childhood love of Nature. Although the fragments of this book had been written for more than fifty years, it was not published until we came to our mountain-top. My husband had always been reluctant to publish these beautiful writings feeling that they would not be understood. To me, these writings were the most exquisite I had ever read, and I insisted that they belonged to the world. Today this personally autographed classic is a collector's item.

We shared our mutual love of Nature's changing

seasons in our daily walks around our beloved mountain until almost the end of his life.

We can more easily "discover" ourselves when we become one with Nature in her great outdoors.

ALL LIVING THINGS RESPOND TO LOVE

Everything, as well as everyone, responds to love. Everyone who loves growing things will tell you stories of how his plants and flowers unfold in healthy loveliness when he *lovingly* cares for them; and when they are neglected how his plants and flowers will droop and die.

I had a beautiful begonia plant that bloomed continuously for six years. Every day I would talk to it and, as I watered it gently and caressingly, the flowers would seem to raise their heads and become more colorful. A journey took me away from this lovely plant and, three days after I left, it died. The same thing happened to several pots of African violets which had bloomed for more than fifteen years. All of these plants had been cared for, but not with the personal love I gave them.

Flowers, plants, and all living things, are like humans—hungry for love. A person who feels the lack of love will often "die" inside. His body may go on living—motion may be there, but the joy of living fades. Lovely Mary Roberts Rinehart said, *"To be needed and wanted by those we love is the nearest we can come to happiness."* Many echo this senti-

51

ment. Flowers and plants—and all living things—desire to be needed and wanted, and to know that they are loved.

A beautiful and sensitive story about a great man who talked with flowers was written by Glenn Clark in his intimate life story of Dr. George Washington Carver. This precious little book which is entitled, *The Man Who Talks With The Flowers,* tells of Dr. Carver's great genius in working with flowers and plants, and how love gave him awareness of the curative and food properties of the simple peanut.

There is so much man discovers when he tends *still* life. Everything and everyone has a place and a purpose, and to discover Life's secrets is to discover your Self.

THE EMOTION OF SELF-REPROACH

One of the most frustrating emotions is self-reproach when one loses a loved one. At the passing of a dear one, almost everyone thinks what else he *might* have done, and if he had only thought of doing this or that, his dear one would never have died. Days, weeks, months, and sometimes years, of self-reproach burn into one's heart and Soul, and this unbearable sense of guilt paralyzes one into inactivity.

It is most important to realize that in these heartbreaking times in our lives we have done everything we knew how to do. Everyone always does the best that he *can* do at his stage of understanding even though what he does may not measure up to what another person may do. Each man's capacity of doing anything is his alone.

To recognize each one's limitations, and to be tolerant of each other's shortcomings, takes years of self-discipline. Sometimes it takes a great shock, or a great tragedy, to teach one the true meaning of tolerance. However, for his own sake, each man must some day learn the tolerance born of understanding. Otherwise, his whole being will be wound up in tensions which will eventually "strangle" him. These tensions will create toxicities which give birth to various illnesses.

When we put the Law of Love into practice, we do not create frustrating experiences that cause self-reproach. Self-reproach can be voided by giving loving service to our fellow man. It is one of life's great lessons that most of us have to learn.

A TEEN-AGER'S GREAT VICTORY

As I was writing this chapter, my mail arrived and I received a letter from a sixteen-year-old girl who has had a great victory over guilt and frustrations. Just over a year ago she was in great trouble.

She is the daughter of a woman who had sunk to very low levels in sex perversions, and other social misdemeanors; and she, herself, was involved in similar practices with a switch-blade gang group. Two of our wonderful married students, who have taken many such young people into their home because of their need of loving help, begged to be allowed to rehabilitate this young girl, knowing that it was only love and understanding that she needed. She had been arrested and placed in several foster homes, but no one had been able to help her. The State authorities were ready to commit her to an institution.

Our students gave her my book entitled *God Will Work With You But Not For You* to read. On their recent visit to Swannanoa, they told me how, for a year, she had read and studied this book until the pages were threadbare. They said she carried the book everywhere, holding it close to her breast, saying, *"This book saved my life. It told me what God really was . . ."*

These people told me that everything about this girl today is a wonderful example of victory over guilt and frustrations.

I was telling this young girl's story to some very dear, loving friends and neighbors, and the daughter said, *"Please send her a copy of your book from us so that she can have her very own copy."* They also expressed the desire to meet her if she ever visited Swannanoa. They wanted to remain anonymous as, of course, this young lady will remain anonymous to you.

Here are the letters just received which she wrote upon receipt of the book. Her own precious words express the depth of her great understanding today.

The first letter is to her loving donors:

"To two lovely people who wanted me to have my own copy of this book, I give my deepest and sincerest thanks and I pray that God's peace will be with you eternally. If it be the will of God I pray that some day I may have the pleasure of meeting you both.

Much love and Prayer.
C. B."

Her letter to me reads as follows:

"It was with great joy that I received your book, 'God Will Work With You But Not For You.' How will I ever be able to thank you enough for this great Message? God has shown me many spiritual truths through this book and it has done a great deal for my soul.

The whole idea of this letter is to thank you and bless you and our Father who gives you all these ideas and words to write in your books, sending words of life and love and encouragement to so many hungry and thirsty people. Yes, truly our God is a great God and I know that He has everything in His hands.

I do not expect you to write to me for I know how busy you must be. Just knowing we share in His great Love is enough for me. I will now close and I pray that God will continue blessing you in His services for Him.

Much love in Him. C. B"

Can you imagine the great joy such letters bring to me? What *greater* joy is there than serving each other? Actually we *all* serve each other in some capacity and in doing so we fulfill ourselves.

ONE MONTH LATER . . .

THE MIRACLE OF LOVE

Surely miracles *do* happen every day of our lives! Even though wonderful things happen each day that tell me of someone's "miraculous" overcomings through the application of these teachings, I *never* fail to feel a deep emotion of gratefulness within me as I open my mail. The tears of pure joy come unrestrainedly from my eyes, and I know the strength and power of the universe to continue with the task which takes my every moment.

I was retyping my manuscript to make it ready for printing, and was about halfway through this very chapter, **Victory Over Guilt And Frustrations,** when the following letter arrived from the wonderful woman who had done so much to make the victory possible of the young girl you have just read about in **A Teen-ager's Great Victory.** Needless to say, the message it contained touched me deeply, not only because of the poignant and glorious story of awakening as to what Love truly *is,* but because I could visualize the same things happening to so many more through their self-inflicted fear and hate.

56

Victory over Guilt and Frustrations

"Dear Lao,

I would like to take this opportunity to share with you what you and your husband's teachings have meant to my life and the life of those God has entrusted to my care. From the age of five I have felt an inner longing and cry for fulfillment and a desire to make God known to the world . . . at the age of thirty I came to a very painful and shocking realization. I did not know God. . . . I could not give forth what I myself did not possess, a consciousness of God. This would seem to be a desolate place to find oneself. . . . Where was I to turn, my family I knew would not understand and I knew no one who shared my convictions. I turned within and cried for truth and a reality of His presence. Several weeks later this desire placed within my hands a copy of Dr. Russell's book, 'The Divine Iliad.' As I read this book my soul became so ecstatic as I was bathed in the light of truth. I became disappointed as the book was drawing to a close as I wanted to go on and on. I then learned of the Home Study Course and your immortal book, 'God Will Work With You But Not For You,' both of which I ordered. These teachings have fed my hungering and thirsting soul and they shall continue to do so as there is an inexhaustible life time supply contained therein for my soul to feast upon.

Through your teachings life began to take on new meaning, given a purpose and directed into a path which will ultimately unfold into full realization of

57

my oneness with God. I would like to share with you one of the many experiences these truths have had upon my life.

Through the realization of life's experiences to be self created and inflicted brought such an inner release that my body sensed a state of weightlessness. The awareness of such a truth, I could now release all those whom I had held in bondage believing them to be the source of my so called afflictions. Of course I now understand it was I who was in bondage. I knew now what the words 'When you shall know the truth, the truth shall set you free,' really meant. I was now free to use my own inner resources; giving myself to that which I desired. Not looking to the world, depending or holding responsible anyone else for its outcome, I found as I placed in motion the laws of your living philosophy as contained in your masterpiece, 'God Will Work With You . . .' that love, peace, joy, and happiness which I sought was contained within and only as they were brought forth into expression were they experienced. Planting the seed of desire to bring forth love into manifestation, God through an inner revelation revealed the channel of expression to be that of children. My first reaction was one of rebellion but I knew that the seed would grow, blossom and bring forth fruit as God worked with me. I then surrendered to His Will and through inspiration He revealed the purpose and plan of His revelation. My husband and I became one in our desire to bring the message of love to children. It would be impossible to relate the immeasurable results that love and the expression of your teachings have had upon the lives of those children God has entrusted to our care. It can, however, be measured to some extent by the influence these children are now having upon others which has been unbelievable. One of these examples I would like to relate later.

Now if I may I would like to share the story of one girl's life as it was before and after she became acquainted with the message of 'God Will Work With You But Not For You.' A year and a half ago a young girl of 14 was brought to our home for the night. The following day she was to be committed to a State Mental Institution. C——— at the age of 11 had become a product of a broken home. Both parents were alcoholics and unbalanced in sex exchange. Due to the lack of proper guidance and the subjection to a totally unbalanced environment and relationships within the home, C——— too, became unbalanced in her thinking, behavior and relationships with society. She became involved many times with the law through her membership with gangs, a pathological liar, a thief and possessed with many psychosomatic ailments. The night she was brought to our home C——— had already made three suicidal attempts and had been placed in five foster homes, all of whom had failed in their attempt to correct either her thinking, behaviour or relationships. According to the State Department of Welfare, the only solu-

tion left was to have her institutionalized. After spending many hours with C——— that evening I sensed she truly desired deliverance and through this desire I knew she had been divinely guided and directed to our home. We felt it to be no accident. Why some may ask? Because through your teachings we had learned the answers and solutions to the problems which had been plaguing and destroying this girl's life. We strongly felt that with both the desire and the solutions at hand we had the victory but it would take time to be brought into manifestation. After making an appeal to the State Department we were granted permission to work with this girl. For many months it did not look good or as if we or she would succeed in our attempt. There were several encounters with the law and society. But our faith and love did not waver because the desire and solution had not disappeared. On one occasion the attending Psychiatrist issued a decree to have C——— placed in either a training school or mental institution. We again begged for mercy for more time as we were now seeing progress that others apparently were not aware of. After this C——— was thoroughly convinced of our love and sincere interest in her life and welfare. When this sense of security was established things began to happen. She first began to share our interest in spiritual matters, reading the literature which was in the home. One day she asked to borrow my book 'God Will . . .' That was the last time I layed my hands on the book for

60

many months. C———— carried the book everywhere she went; the doctors, swimming, visiting or on vacation. Wherever you would find C———— there would be the book. She has read the book several times and it would be impossible for me to put into words how C———— feels regarding the message of this book. She now has her own copy and lends it out to her friends. Her life is a living testimony of what the message has meant. She has been completely delivered of all psychosomatic ailments and no recurrence of her apparent problems which had this girl bound for so many years. Her life is now filled with expressions of love, giving of herself to all those she comes in contact. She has become a great blessing to others and a living, inspiring example of what this message can do for those who will apply it as a living philosophy. When C———— doctor saw her several months ago she declared with a tear in her eye, "I was wrong, the R————s were right and I have begun to believe in miracles.

We believe the secret of success of this your immortal message lies in its transference from one to another. We have seen this exemplified through the children in their relationships with friends. My husband has seen the lives of those in his office so completely changed as they absorbed this message of love. One of whom had been in prison has now turned his home over to unwanted children; others who thought only of getting and taking have been so completely changed in their thinking. This was not accomplished through words but as my husband lived this message from day to day. I would like to inject at this time that up until several years ago my husband would not have thought of sharing his home with others or express love to others. He thought this was for only those of your own household.

I would like to now share just one of the many examples of those whose lives have been influenced through contact with the children here. A girl of nineteen had been taught and preached to all her life concerning the principles of Christianity but had never seen any real examples of it applied to life. . . . The first time she came for a visit she was rather uneasy which I learned later was due to the fact she had heard we were some of those so called religious people. However, much to her surprise no one preached to her and she has been coming back ever since declaring that the influence in the home keeps drawing her back. This influence she declares is the love and concern she feels and sees expressed among each member of the family for one another. She comes as often as she can to be with the children and in her own words 'to be renewed and refreshed.' Through the influence of love she has become so burdened for others. This very night as I am writing this letter I heard she spent the day ministering in love to many who were in great need.

As I write this letter we in no way profess to have reached perfect balanced interchange in all our relationships but we are striving day by day to become living testimonies to this your message. We know from experience that it works as it has brought love, peace, joy and happiness both to ourselves and others.

What else can I say but to praise God for His messengers of light which has brought the light of truth which if obeyed will set men free.

With great love
A. R."

LOVE'S VICTORY

LOVE can open all doors and heal *all* wounds. No words of mine could tell you this with greater clarity than the words of the above letter.

I shall not rewrite what I had already written under **A Teen-ager's Great Victory** because this heartwarming and Soul-stirring letter tells its own inspiring story of battles won between the *Soul and the Senses*. The magnificent victories of those who now understand the true meaning of The Message which Jesus gave when He was on earth—*Love Ye One Another*—foretell a victory for *all* mankind.

NOW IS ETERNITY

Every *moment* of your life is a new beginning, for *now is eternity*. Since this moment *is* all we have—and will ever have—let us start this moment to weave our magic carpet of Love and Romance. All guilts, frustrations, fears, sorrows, and hatreds, have been voided—as in truth they have. We are going to unfold a new and glorious chapter in our lives built on Love, Truth, Honesty, Kindness, and Loyalty— all the qualities we cannot *see*, but we can *know*. Upon these Soul qualities we can weave a beautiful pattern for our lives.

First, we know that everything that happened, that we can see, was a *thought* which we cannot see, but we can know. Our desire is to build a temple of light and love of our bodies with these qualities that come from *within* us.

Patiently, we shall daily express these qualities as we pursue our daily tasks. When we get up in the morning, we shall be grateful for another wonderful day of sharing. We shall be in a state of constant expectancy of wonderful things happening to us during the day. And what *is* a wonderful thing? Truly the *most* wonderful experience every day is to share happy moments with each other. All of the *things* on earth cannot give us happiness if we do not have each other.

When you wake up with a smile on your lips, you meet the day with a smile. It is hard for others not to smile *with* you. Your joys are multiplied in all those whom you contact the livelong day. Every thing that you do is tinged with love and joy. Therefore, whatever you do is well done. Work done with love is always well done, gives *you* inner satisfaction, and pleases the one to whom you have given service.

Service with love brings man his greatest fulfillment.

School work done with joy is also well done, and gives the student a deep sense of inner satisfaction and pride. *Satisfaction within one's self gives one confidence in one's self.*

One who begins the day with joy and love in his heart brings into being a happy day, for joy is self-bestowed just as misery is self-inflicted. At the end of a happy day, one has a sense of well being and anticipation for another day of joy on the morrow. With this continual sense of well being, events come into one's life that bring an ecstasy too deep for words. Living in a constant state of joyous anticipation and ecstasy, is being "in tune with the Infinite."

When we work knowingly *with* our Creator, we live in harmony with the laws of the universe. The law of attraction is an inviolate law. Our desire for a true mate will bring that true mate to us. Live life *worthily,* and that one who is *worthy* of YOU will come TO you.

Every man is important to every other man, for each is born to fill the need of the other.

YOUR NIGHTLY REBORNING

The following excerpt, from my beloved's prayer for the night, seems a fitting close to this chapter:

Love

"My day is done. The portals of Thy night encircle me. The Peace of Thy Rest encompasseth me.

To Thy heavens decentrate me, O my Father, and thus renew me, for reconcentrating upon Mother Earth for one more day of manifesting Thee.

I feel Thee coming, ever coming, to sever Spirit of me from its sensed clay to take back to Source of me for reborning with its sensed clay image at the dawn.

Destroy Thou that ego which is not Thee in me. Let my Self be Thy Self in me.

Exalt Thou me. Take Thou me unto Thy high mountain-top in ecstasy, that my morrow may reflect Thy glory in manifesting Thee.

Within the Oneness of Thy Spirit let me find surcease from action, as waves of ocean find surcease in ocean's calm.

Upon my heart those unsolved problems of my day are plainly writ for solving in Thy Light for my new day.

Re-attune the discords of my mal-patterned thinking with the harmonies of Thy balanced rhythmic thinking.

Immunize Thou my man-formed clay from toxins of un-rhythmic pulsing begot from unbalanced thinking and from wrong action.

Void Thou the fears of my unknowing of the Light when my path is thereby made dark.

Thus reinspire me with more knowing of Thy purpose that I may more worthily fulfill Thy purpose.

66

Enfold Thou my spirit, O heavenly night. Enshroud Thou me in thy veiled mysteries, and deliver my resurrected clay to dawn, again renewed, again made whole.

Reborn Thou me in Thy Consciousness that I may again sing the glad song of one more cosmic day in Light of new knowing."

As we rest in the stillness of sleep, we recharge our bodies and Mind for a new day of victorious achievement. Each dawn gives birth to a new beginning that is our very own.

CHAPTER IV

The Magic Power of Sex

Man and woman are forever seeking balanced mates, for they intuitively know that with and through each other they have a greatly multiplied power of expression. The scientific explanation of this multiplied power lies in the fact that not only their bodies but their thinking, also, becomes polarized.

This polarization can only come from sex matehood between man and woman. That is why homosexuality has a weakening effect rather than a strengthening one. It naturally follows that lesbianism has the same weakening effect.

Male and female sex intercourse brings polarization to *balanced* mates. There is a great vitalizing force for both when true love has given birth to the sex desire.

When a male has sexual relations with another male, or a female with a female, there is not a polarization, but rather a depolarization, which has a *devitalizing* effect. Naturally, the thinking of such people is also unbalanced.

In one of our lessons in our *Home Study Course in*

68

Universal Law, Natural Science and Living Philosophy is the following on POLARITY:

"The basic law of Creation demands equality in all interchange between the pairs of units in all Creation which are engaged in such interchange. . . .

Nature will not tolerate any violation of sex-balance whatsoever and that is why we see anguish, disease, frustrations, divorces, bankruptcies and many forms of unhappiness around about us everywhere in small scale, and hatreds, enmities and wars in large scale. All of the troubles of all the world lie in that one cause—breach of the law of polarity which upsets the balance of every transaction between DIVIDED PAIRS.

When a transaction between divided pairs fails to UNITE those divided pairs, unhappiness is as sure to follow as night follows day.

A seesaw is an excellent example of polarity or sex-division. That is why we choose this example. It is important that you realize and recognize that similarity. A seesaw divides the one balance of its fulcrum into two extended balances which must be equally balanced in order to unite and repeat."

OUR SEX DRIVES

When a man and a woman's desires are strong, they can mistake sex for love. Our emotional hunger for sex could be likened to a strong desire for food.

69

This "hunger," scientifically explained, is that the one desire of separated male and female particles or masses is to unite to void their separateness. Upon this formula our electric universe of motion is founded.

To understand our sex drive is of equal importance to both girls and boys. It is important to save both from a sense of *guilt* and *frustration*. Fear is often born of frustration, and then it is a short step to hate. Frustrations make us introspective, and then fear unbalances our thinking; we begin to blame others for the things and incidents we, ourselves, have created. Then we actually hate ourselves for so doing, and the chain reaction sets in.

In our book, *Scientific Answer to Sex Promiscuity*, my husband states:

"Different kinds of food produce different effects upon the body structure and pattern. Likewise, different kinds of sex have different effects upon the body structure and pattern.

More than that, sex has different effects upon the intellectual and moral thinking processes as well.

It has been said that 'a man is what he thinks'; also that 'a man is what he eats.'

To this should be added, 'a man is what his sex practice and sex ideals make of him.'

Sex practice and ideals of sex determine the standards of both body and mind. One will inevitably ascend, or descend, physically, mentally and spiritually through one's sex practice."

70

EVERY INTERCHANGE IS A SEX INTERCHANGE

Every interchange is a sex interchange. When a man and woman *talk* together, this is a *mental sex interchange.* Powerful ideas are born of mental sex interchange when a man and woman are *balanced mental mates.* That is why men and women should work together—mentally—because they would then know the ecstasy of balanced mental matehood.

The greatest ecstasy I have ever known was when my beloved husband and I wrote together. One day we were going over our book, *The One-World Purpose,* and discovered that neither of us could claim even one sentence as being written by one or the other. Each sentence consisted of one word of his and one word mine, so *one* were we in Mind. To experience such sharing is rare, but it need not be. O, the ecstasy of such sharing. It truly goes beyond any physical ecstasy, however great, that one can ever know. When we reach this point of ONENESS, we know our universal oneness with all life. This means freedom from self-bondage.

THE EFFECTS OF SEX PRACTICES

My husband said in regard to the effects of sex practices in his book, *Scientific Answer to Sex Promiscuity:*

"Sex practice can be the most spiritually uplifting or the most mentally and physically defiling thing in

71

one's life, according to one's ideals concerning sex thinking, or lack of them. The greatest injury from promiscuous sex relations lies in the fact that each person has his own 'wave length' or 'number'— and his own wave pattern—which he has created from his own thinking. Promiscuous sex relations affect both by undermining both.

Each is benefited if the wave patterns are harmonious or injured if the electrical wave patterns are too greatly opposed. Few realize that every cell in the body, plus the nature of the blood stream, is permanently affected—for better or worse—by sex relations.

The sex relation unifies two close mates but badly distorts electrically unbalanced ones.

Years of hard climbing toward one's spiritual goal can be nullified in one brief costly hour of thoughtlessness in violating this most holy relationship between the sexes.

Just as wrong sex practices can defile a life, so, likewise, can it defile a whole civilization.

The ever thoughtless average human thinks that sexual promiscuity leaves no damaging effects unless one of the participants is diseased. Mr. Average Man would be shocked to learn that the very Self-pattern of his racial ideal, his emotion, his blood stream, his individual ideal and his very character is degenerated by choosing the wrong mate and by every promiscuous sexual experience."

BOY AND GIRL SEX

Often a sense of guilt and frustration affects a boy because, after he has satisfied his physical desires, he realizes that he has become caught in a web which threatens his freedom. Youth, above all, desires freedom. It is not prepared for responsibility. A boy of seventeen is usually far younger in attitude than a girl of seventeen. Generally, boys mature much later than girls.

All too often, when boys and girls marry very young, they have a sense of missing something—as indeed they often do. There are always exceptions to the rule, naturally. When we find two people celebrating their Golden Wedding Anniversary in their late sixties, or early seventies, it usually signifies that theirs has been one of those wonderfully successful early marriages.

The sex drive in a man is a different thing from the sex drive in a woman. *Man gives love to get sex, and woman gives sex to get love.* The basic difference in sex and love, as I said before, is that sex is of the senses and is, therefore, a *transitory sensation.* Love is a Soul-quality—not of the senses but of Mind— and is, therefore, an *eternal quality.*

TIME ELEMENT FOR MARRIAGE

The desire of Love is to know oneness mentally as well as physically. That is why there is always that faint disappointment after sex intercourse unless there is true love. The senses *alone* can *never* satisfy. For this reason, the period before marriage is of utmost importance in "discovering" each other's mental and spiritual attitudes. Balance, which alone sustains happiness, can only be maintained when these attitudes are alike.

Those precious days are the ones that we need in order to be more certain that we can spend the rest of our lives sharing in life's drama of living. Those are the days of deep contemplation of each other's thoughts and habits, days in which to consider whether the one who seems so physically exciting would make a life companion for *everyday sharing* of the incidents which make up our way of life.

The question to ask one's self is, is *this* the man— or woman—with whom I could share my innermost thoughts and desires? Could I really be *myself* with him—or her? Could I share my disappointments and hurts as well as my joys with this boy—or girl? Most important of all—do we have the same standard of IDEALS? These are vital questions to ask one's self. If you cannot find a big "YES" within yourself to these questions, do not become involved physically to the point where you cannot think at all. It *is* difficult to think when passions are high. All you can think of then is possessing that one's body. In the heat of emotion you *believe* it is love when, in reality, it is desire for body sensation to void sex tensions.

74

THE QUALITIES WE DESIRE

The one and only desire of Love is to *give,* and a desire to *take* in sex is not truly love. If a boy loves a girl, he desires always to cherish and protect her. This being so, he must first respect her. When a girl allows herself to be used in sex without love, she loses *her* self-respect, and then frustrations set in within herself and within the boy friend, also. We are all innately idealistic, and we are all searching for the ideal mate, the one who is truly our other half. It is important to build our relationships on respect, which is admiration, and this can come only through a sharing in Mind.

My husband used to say to me, *"I do not know whether I love you more or admire you more."* When we are very young, such a remark often "floors" us, because we want so much to be *loved* more than anything else. We seem to want to be loved for superficial qualities when we are young but, as we become more mature in our thinking, we realize that it is the love born of respect and admiration for the Soul qualities that gives us the kind of love which lasts forever.

I often tell groups of teen-agers, *"If you want to marry a prince, make yourself into a princess."* In other words, if you want to marry someone very *special,* make yourself into a very *special* person.

What constitutes a special person? Not body alone, certainly. A special person is one who cannot only look beautiful, but be interesting and entertaining to be with. And above all, be beautiful on the *inside,* which means be loving and kind and helpful in a million *little* ways.

BEAUTY ATTRACTS

In all and through all you do express beauty. Beauty *always* attracts; ugliness detracts. Beauty is the light of love. It comes from within you, and shines through your eyes like a million stars. That light which shines through your eyes comes from your innermost thoughts. *You are what you think.* Your face and whole body reflect what you think and do. Beauty reflects freedom from all that is unlovely. All that is unlovely will bind you in chains of steel which will hold you a prisoner from love.

THE QUALITIES THE WORLD IS CRYING FOR

Love, Truthfulness, Honesty, Loyalty, Kindness —all these Soul qualities give you freedom. The whole world is crying for these qualities. Lack of them gives birth to the crime waves which are now sweeping the world.

SUICIDE, CRIME AND SEX UNBALANCE

The sex urge is the strongest motivating force of all life. For this reason, it must be understood for what it is. People all over the world are living in fear today because of unexplainable sex crimes. We find no explanation for the *motives* of many of these tragic crimes.

As I write this book, riots and strikes fill the headlines. News stories tell of "killings" by young men who have been considered fine and upstanding individuals. The ever-increasing tensions through seemingly uncontrollable crimes are creating such widespread fear that life for many is becoming unbearable.

How many people realize that the root cause for most of the rising crime is *sex unbalance!*

There is a scientific explanation for many useless crimes. That is *why* the scientific aspect of sex *must* be taught and practiced throughout our lives. *Only that which we understand do we put into practice.*

I will quote again from my husband's book, *Scientific Answer to Sex Promiscuity*. In his chapter on **Sex Unbalance** he explains *what* causes a person to commit violent murder. He says as follows:

"Every separate cell of the body has a direct connection with the brain. If all the body cells oscillate in unequal pulsations, imagine the terrific damage unknowingly done to the nervous system by so huge a multiplication of unbalanced messages reaching the brain from so many unequally balanced body cells.

The urge of body cells upon the brain is sometimes so much greater than the control of the brain upon the cells that a man's will power is often controlled entirely by this urge of the body cells. For

77

instance a man whose brain tells him he must not and does not wish to kill, but he kills because of an 'uncontrollable urge.' He cannot help it. He is but an automaton obeying distorted messages sent to his brain by body cells which become frightfully distorted in pattern.

It is, therefore, of vital importance in the building of the pattern of the individual that the cell urge be under the control of the conscious Spirit in man rather than in the cells of the body. This can only be possible if the electrical interchange between sex mates is so equal that one can forget his body entirely as all geniuses do. Freedom from body is necessary for those who do creative work. Any inequality or unlikeness whatsoever leaves a residue of electrical unbalance which evidences itself in many intensities, from slightly neurotic conditions arising from the unbalance due to repressions, pessimism, fanaticism and insanity, to committing violent murder.

These residual unbalances accumulate in time and force their victims to seek balance at any cost. The insane asylums have all too many of these sex dissatisfied and abnormal mismatings."

I trust the brief scientific explanation of the sex principle in this chapter will help you to understand how sex motivates your thoughts and actions. *The sex principle is the electric force of all life in motion.* When we learn to *control* this force through Mind-thinking, instead of purely physical desire, our sexual

78

practices lift us to the heights of mental inspiration.

YOU CAN BECOME A HUMAN DYNAMO

When you understand the extent of the power which lies within you, and learn to control that power instead of allowing it to control you, you can become a human dynamo. Ignorance of the laws which govern us has brought agony to many unsuspecting human beings, and that is why one must ever seek for greater knowledge and understanding.

The creative person is strongly sexed, and it is most important that he or she finds a balancing mate. When this genius-type finds true love, his contributions to his fellow man, and to the world, are very great and of lasting value.

Not only is the contribution of creative genius greatly accelerated, but every type of man and woman contributes far more to life with balanced matehood. The desire to *give* happiness to all is greatly increased. Also, any work performed by those who know balance in sex is done with far greater joyousness, and everyone benefits by the harmony of love in action.

THE TYPE OF MATE FOR *YOU*

To define *balance* for you in your sex interchangings, let us consider the type best suited to you. It is obvious that you need a mate with whom you can *feel and be yourself*. You can only be *yourself*

79

with one to whom you can express your inner desires without constant opposition.

Opposition of ideals and desires creates tensions, and sex intercourse can only be ideal when both are relaxed and completely natural with each other. In this state of oneness is the rapture of true matehood.

When two people have opposite desires, they obviously cannot live happily together, for sex is but a small part of living and loving together. As I mentioned previously, it is the twenty-three hours of sharing that are of *first* import; for if they are harmonious, the other hour of physical sharing can be ecstatic.

Balance in one's sex life can only be retained when there is a *balanced* mental and physical sharing. After the first sex hunger of a physical attraction has been satisfied, there *must* be a strong mental attraction to keep alive the physical attraction. In the first flush of physical attraction, one cannot remind oneself of this fact too often.

This is what I mean by balance in regard to your sex life. You cannot "make love" twenty-four hours a day, but the sex relations of two people who can harmoniously share twenty-three hours a day can be so ecstatic—because their bodies are so balanced— that their whole attitude to life is more loving and tolerant, and they take this love and tolerance into their every action the livelong day.

Yesterday, a woman visitor was telling me about

her sons. One was twenty-seven when he married, and had not been a very thoughtful son. However, after his marriage to a loving and kind girl, he changed so much and brought great joy to his parents' hearts. She also has a younger son, and said he was basically good but, when he was away in college without their loving influence, he did things he would never do at home. She said that *"All he needed was a push in the right direction to make him satisfied and happy with himself. The RIGHT girl could do this for him."*

We *all* need the love and inspiration of that right *one*. While we may make mistakes and create our own agonies, we can void our mistakes and go forward seeking that balancing mate that our inner being forever desires.

AS WE START THE DAY

I continually stress the fact that a happy home life will bring into being a happy world. A man and woman take the attitude, with which they start their day, into everything they do and say the whole day through.

As I mentioned before, our divorce rate tells its own story of unhappy homes. This means that before these people separated, they were leaving each other in the mornings without *love* in their hearts and thoughts. They both injected their unhappiness into all they did and said. Their faces reflected this inner unhappiness, and this did not attract others to them.

If either one happened to be in sales, he would not project the enthusiasm necessary to make a good sale. To be a good salesman, one *must* be genuinely enthusiastic about what one is selling, otherwise one cannot create a desire to purchase in the customer's mind.

Without enthusiasm, there is no joy in any kind of work; and whatever work one is doing suffers accordingly. If you are an office worker, you will make mistakes which can be costly to your employer or to yourself.

If you are an assembly line worker, you do not put the parts together as precisely as you should, and the machine soon breaks down. We have practically all had this experience with new machines today—and most people wonder why. *Only work done with love is done perfectly.*

If you are a teacher, children are quick to pick up your mood. They will become restless and inattentive, and you will become full of tensions.

People are talking about tensions today little realizing that they, themselves, are adding to these tensions when they become worried and irritated by the self-created problems of today's world. We all contribute to these tensions knowingly—or unknowingly—when we leave home and our loved ones in a "bad" mood.

What is the answer? I repeat—*live love by giving love to all that you do,* from the mundane chores of dusting, or emptying the garbage, to writing a poem.

It is not what we *do* that is half as important as *how* we approach our task of doing it. Life is not easy. It will never be easy, but we can make it a glorious adventure if our desire is strong enough to give service with love.

Let us make this a happy world. *Every* man is the world, and every home multiplies itself into the world-home.

THE ENVIRONMENT YOU CREATE

We are all the sum total of our experiences. Your life today is largely what *you* have made it. Our environments express ourselves. As children, our environment expresses our parents' thinking, but gradually we break away from their environment and create our own. We start doing this as soon as we enter school. Our friends and associates make up our environment. Two children from the same home often create entirely different environments when they leave the parental home. It is the difference in character which influences the creating of different environments.

Your friends make up an important part of your life. *They* create the incidents in your life with you. These can be good and constructive experiences, or they can be destructive ones. Therefore, one should be careful in one's choice of friends.

Choose friends with whom you can follow through on creative ideas. The Junior Chamber of Commerce and Future Farmers of America groups are excellent follow-up groups of Boy Scout groups. The Future Homemakers of America are also excellent follow-up groups for Girl Scouts. I have had heart-warming experiences when speaking to Junior Chambers of Commerce, Future Farmers of America and the Future Homemaking groups.

There are many fine organizations today that young men and women can become an active part of. We all need an outlet for creative ideas, and we need to express these creative ideas to know inner satisfaction. As I stated before, inner satisfaction creates confidence within one's self. This inner satisfaction is very important, for it attracts a sweetheart with similar thinking and accomplishment. Therein lies the key to complete balance in matehood, and this gives birth to the true and lasting romance of LOVE.

SEX SUBLIMATION

When we were nearing the completion of our book, *Scientific Answer to Sex Promiscuity,* we added the following conclusion to clarify the fact that it was not necessary to have physical sex before one could know balance.

"It must, however, always be borne in mind that all relations between opposite sexes are sex relations; and that, as life progresses, the interchanging relationship becomes primarily mental and spiritual— less and less physical—the mental and spiritual sublimating the physical.

The Magic Power of Sex

Many men and women, who, by circumstances of obligation to parents, or through death, and other causes, are unable to marry, are successful in leading balanced lives through their interchange in thought, and by association with those of the opposite sex.

Life is divided into three cycles—the early life is almost completely physical—middle life mental— and the latter part of life, spiritual. It is during these three cycles that one desires a balancing mate to fill his emotional needs, whether physical, mental or spiritual. But it must always be remembered that the balancing is electrical, since all emotions are of the senses and, therefore, are electric.

All electric relations are sexual relations. So, I repeat, unless there is an electric balance the creative urge lacks the necessary stimulus which comes through the stillness of balance."

When creative people are engrossed in objects of their creation, their great sex drive is sublimated. Sex in the physical sense is not uppermost in the thoughts of an inspired person when he is creating.

In early or teen-age years prior to marriage, this strong sex drive can, likewise, be sublimated in creative work, sports or other activities, which use up the strong desires of the body. And there is not anything that can bring such a satisfying sense of well-being to us as accomplishment.

A wonderful example of such accomplishment was when my husband spent a weekend as a guest of

Sir Thomas Lipton on his yacht. While the other guests were enjoying the usual festivities, my husband was sculpturing a plaque in clay of Sir Thomas. We have a lovely bronze of this plaque on one of our glass-topped exhibition tables at Swannanoa.

It was because Walter Russell utilized every moment creatively and constructively that he accomplished so much, and was universally known as "The Modern Leonardo da Vinci." You will also read in Glenn Clark's story of his life, *The Man Who Tapped the Secrets of the Universe,* how he introduced figure skating to this country, and held the championship for figure skating in the United States for four years. At the time he held the championship, he was forty-five to forty-nine years of age. He skated until he was well into his seventies. Many people tell me they remember seeing him skating at Rockefeller Center. It was his one regret that I never saw him skate. He was seventy-four when we met, and had only stopped skating the year before—and then only because his writing and scientific work took every moment of his time.

One does not necessarily have to create a *masterpiece* in the arts, or win a prized trophy in sports. When I was in my teens, I painted water colors, and would never go to bed until I had finished the picture. For two or three years, I spent my evenings painting; and I remember the deep satisfaction that was mine, when I at last finished the picture, and went to bed. I remember that, one year, I sold the pictures and earned sufficient money to pay for my own lovely holiday in the summer.

There are countless ways to sublimate the sex urge, and the greatest one is in serving others. There are so many people in need of help, shut-ins who need little bits of shopping done, women left alone who cannot afford gardeners and who need their lawns mowed, and parents who have lost sons and daughters in wars or accidents. In serving our fellow man, we do not have time to think of *how we feel*. We forget ourselves as we give in service, and always we, in turn, know an inner joyousness in the doing. *Thus is love given and regiven in balanced measure.*

THE MAGIC POWER OF SEX

Every man and every woman desires to know the ecstasy of *oneness*. We seek it eternally, knowing intuitively that our power is multiplied, as indeed it is. The multiplied power of *balanced* matehood is the greatest power that man and woman can ever know, for in the voidance of each other's physical desires is complete balance of motion. The united pair become wholly Mind as that balance occurs.

All energy comes from Mind; therefore, the balanced idea, which springs from complete voidance of physical motion, is the ultimate in power of Mind-expression. This indeed is THE MAGIC POWER OF SEX.

CHAPTER V

Why Many Teen-age Marriages Fail

The reason why many teen-age marriages fail is the same reason that *any* marriage fails. The cause is the same no matter what the age or the circumstance. And what is that cause? *The cause is lack of love.*

The percentage of failures of teen-age marriages is high because it is a period in life when the *physical* senses are predominant.

An *understanding* of these inner driving forces can help all ages to know themselves better, and also what motivates their actions and reactions.

Let us go back to those days, weeks, months, and sometimes years, before marriage, when desire for physical romance was so strong you felt you must die if it did not soon come to you. Desire for "oneness" is so powerful a force that your every action seems to be governed by it. When we see other girls and boys "in love," we want this same state for ourselves so strongly that we are willing to sacrifice our inner ideals of a sweetheart just to "belong" to someone.

When we compromise with our ideals, we are taking the first step to failure in romance and marriage. Failure in romance and marriage—or in any other experience—stems from compromise with the one inviolate principle of Balance.

In settling for less than the ideal we build of a mate, it means we have accepted one who does not fulfill the Law of Balance for us. He or she is too different in thinking and basic desires. If you enjoy poetry, music, and the beauty of nature, and your prospective sweetheart does not enjoy these things which feed your Soul, this builds a residue of unbalance in your sharing. This will eventually lead to discord in your interchanges, however physically exciting the contact of your *bodies* may be.

When we at long last understand that it is the mental interchange that keeps the physical exciting and beautiful, we shall not have the broken marriages, in any age bracket, that we have today.

There is not anything on this earth that can—or will—separate two people who find that physical, mental, and spiritual balance in each other; for this is the balance known as True Love. *All* people seek this balance whether they are aware of it or not.

THE IMPORTANCE OF TIME

When girl meets boy—or boy meets girl—there needs to be a period of romancing before the engagement. It takes a little time to be sure one has found the mate one's heart and soul desires. Emotions can blind even the wisest person to a true valuation of another. It is the every-moment harmonious relationship we all desire—and must have—for a happy *life* relationship. This does not mean that *every* moment with your loved one will be ecstatic. There are times when the greatest lovers in the world are at variance with each other. When people have definite and strong characters, they are bound to have heated discussions at times; but with a true mate there is an underlying sense of love, respect, and understanding. Unless there are these underlying qualities, there always comes a time when "love flies out of the window," and a heart is left in the desolation of loneliness.

I received a telephone call from a woman telling me the sad story of her teen-age daughter's broken marriage. This eighteen-year-old girl had been married about one year. After a six-month pregnancy, she had lost her baby, and a few weeks later her husband told her he did not love her any more. She returned to her parents a very sad, lonely little girl. This is a story that is all too familiar today, and one that need not happen if there were a greater understanding of life itself. This is why we need to know ourselves so that when tragedy strikes, our *aloneness* does not paralyze us with fear of the unknown. No one's life is all honey. Storms, heartache, and tragedy go hand in hand with sunshine, happiness, and every material success.

This is also why it is necessary for *time* to test our

emotional attraction for each other. The qualities which hold a man and woman together are the qualities you do not see or *feel* through your senses (emotions) but you *KNOW* them through your Mind.

THE SEX IMPULSE

First, let us consider the emotional reaction when boy meets girl. There is a stirring of the senses, and a desire to caress and kiss the desired. It is the instinctive desire of mating. *It is the impulse of life itself, for this is a sexed-electric universe.* Without the sex impulse, there would be no life or vegetation on this earth. It is the basic underlying and motivating force of *all* that is in our universe.

It is not the so-called sex problems that break up marriages. As I explained in the first chapter, **Love's Phantasy,** sex is but an *effect* of love. That is why we must understand *what* love really is, so that our sex lives can be not only successful, but grow more and more ecstatic and wonderful as time teaches us how to know and express love.

EVERYONE HAS TO MAKE ADJUSTMENTS

When two young people marry, they truly believe their marriage will last forever. Their love is warm, young, and very vital. When they find the strain and tensions of everyday living creating inharmonies in their relationship, they feel the world has come to an end. The love they once dreamed about seems far, far away.

It takes great maturity of thought to live happily together. Even for those who have the completeness of deep mental and spiritual interchange, continued harmony is a challenge. Each person has to find and know *himself* before he can know and understand another. When at long last he does begin to understand himself, he becomes more tolerant of another's little idiosyncrasies, or ways. Then, rather than love dying, it grows and grows, and life becomes ever more precious in its sharings.

When we are young, we want the constant attention of our loved one. We are hungry for the physical touch of a loved one's hand. If we do not have as much attention as we feel that we should, we feel we are not loved. Irritations set up barriers, and then misunderstandings follow.

HEART TO HEART TALKS CAN SAVE A MARRIAGE

If two young people would "talk things out" quietly, when they are first married, many marriages would be brought into balance. *Living love* is a different story from voicing words of love. However, *living love* can be far more romantic than listening to all the sweet words of love. *Living love* means giving of yourself in all you do. All through this book you will find this one principle of love—GIVING. You cannot get away from it, for love is all there is in all our great and beautiful world—and WHAT IS LOVE, BUT *GIVING?*

Returning to that first year of marriage—when the honeymoon is over, and after all the words of endearment and protestations of eternal love have seared themselves into your Soul, and after bodies have spent themselves in passions fulfilled—this is the time when the *real* romance of living is yours: yours to mold into a satisfying life of oneness, or yours to tear asunder in the passions of misunderstandings.

To try to build a life of love everlasting without an understanding of love, is like trying to drive through the country without a road map.

When people marry with the sole idea that in so doing they will be *given* happiness, they begin life together with the greatest deterrent to continued romance. We should *never* marry with the thought of anyone making *us* happy, but rather with the thought of what *we can give to make that one happy.* There is a world of difference in these two desires.

No one else can ever truly make *us* happy. *First,* we must be happy *within ourselves,* and then we are ready to *share* happiness. Being happy within yourself means you understand what Love is. We cannot TAKE love—we can only GIVE love. Those who have reached this stage of understanding have experienced all the trials and tribulations of life's unfolding.

Life is never easy for anyone, even though outside

appearances may deem otherwise. This is another reason why early marriages so often fail.

Let us consider the first heated argument that follows the blissful honeymoon, when all we had to think about was ourselves and the feelings of our loved one. We return to the home, which is to be our own little paradise on earth, and we believe those ecstatic moments of the honeymoon will go on and on forever. We come down to earth with a bump when we start the unfamiliar task of housekeeping. Anything that is unfamiliar is difficult at first. It takes us longer to do, and tires us more. Some of the chores seem very unromantic, and either one or the other starts grumbling about those unromantic chores.

There is not anything that can kill romance as fast as a whining attitude towards doing the things about a home that *must* be done. Soon the whining creeps into all conversations, and how can a man—or woman—want to make love to a grumbler!

Much could be written on this subject, for more marriages fail because of the petty aggravations of domestic life than perhaps anything else. It all boils down to one thing—attitude in how we face the *living* of life. Meeting all life's challenges with a loving attitude keeps romance bright and fresh. All the little seemingly unpleasant chores are in reality chores of loving service. They *give* us the opportunity to serve each other, and *to serve each other is our great purpose on earth*. Discover this great secret of giving service, and you have discovered the *secret* of a happy life. "Happy" is really not the best word to describe the inner joy that comes from service with love—"ecstasy" better describes it.

The first year of married life is often not the easiest, or happiest. Each one has to make adjustments and, when both are very definite characters there has to be much giving—and understanding— on both sides.

How many people have divorced, and then married another, only to find that they have to cope with another set of differences in their mates? However, in a second marriage there is often more tolerance and understanding; so they are better equipped to make a success of their marriage. Also, they are usually more mature in years, and know the importance of mental companionship.

BALANCE IS THE KEY TO MARRIED BLISS

There are many challenges for two people to meet in marriage. However, "love will always find a way." It is always a case of understanding each other's desires. There are women who, because of centuries of women's suppression, feel they have to be dogmatic to make themselves heard. This creates a competitive attitude with their husband's, rather than a cooperative and balancing one.

A brilliant and dedicated woman attended some

of my lectures this spring, and because her letter might help other women who have found themselves in a like state of mind, I will give you her entire letter. Because of her dedication to her fellow man, I know she will be happy to have you share this with me.

"*Lao dear,*

Your philosophy really works when it is lived. Since I read 'GOD WILL WORK WITH YOU BUT NOT FOR YOU,' my whole life has changed —and consequently, the lives of my family.

As I told you last Sunday, I received my AB Degree in philosophy from the University of C——— in 1942, and have studied philosophy and metaphysics ever since; but, as far as I'm concerned, I could throw away every book I've ever read now that I have 'GOD WILL WORK WITH YOU BUT NOT FOR YOU.'

During the week between the day I heard you speak in Menlo Park and the following Sunday, when I went to hear you again and took my husband with me, we turned off our TV and bought a stereo to flood our home with music of the Spirit.

Oh, it isn't just the music that has made such a change in our home, Lao—it's the relationship between B——— and me that has made the difference, now that I realize through your book, that I no longer have to compete with him. For the first time in my life, I really want to be a WOMAN, because

96

your book has shown me that WOMAN can express her Self just as much as MAN—if not more!

'BALANCE' is the magic word. Always before, I was fighting for equal rights as a woman; this led to competition, and let loose a destructive force. In order to excel over my husband, it became necessary to belittle him in everything that he did. Little did I know, until you came long, that there could never be a balanced, constructive power in our home so long as I exalted myself above my mate.

I know full well that the magic of a realization can wear off as the days grow numerous between the time of the inspiration and the time of the first little, annoying 'difference' that is bound to occur in any marriage; but this, too, we have weathered since you were here. After ten days of ecstasy, it was all the more crushing when the little difference came up. Although the unbalance was ever so slight, we could hardly stand it this time.

However, having your philosophy to cling to was like being able to grab onto a redwood tree when one is about to slide off the path and down a steep slope. We caught ourselves before we made it necessary to climb all the way back up the incline, and are walking on the firm path hand in hand once again— in balance.

As I told you last Sunday, I'm so enthusiastic about this philosophy that I would like to help you spread it to every corner of the world—and my husband is 100% behind me.

Love

B. and I both thank you for showing us the way to change our lives through BALANCE, Lao. I will look forward to hearing from you as soon as you've had a chance to catch your breath after your return from your speaking tour.

With deep forest love,
B. P. B."

I trust this beautifully expressed letter helps someone reading this book. Our students always appreciate sharing the thoughts of other students, for they say it helps them to identify themselves with the strengths and weaknesses of others. Through this sharing, they know they are not alone in their climb to the heights of perfection. We have literally thousands of magnificent and inspiring letters such as the few I am sharing with you in this book. Some day they shall be made up into books, for no story is as stirring as a *true* story; and these thousands of letters, which we have on file, are a saga of love and life in action.

KNOW YOU NEVER WORK ALONE

Returning to the mundane things that "floor" many women, I recall a student writing me once that she "just hated making beds." She said she had to make five each day. I wrote her saying that she did not make those beds alone since Mind—which is God—made them with her. I explained how Mind sent a message to her brain, and her brain sent a message to her hands; so, in truth, God made the beds *with* her. She could not get tired, therefore, for energy comes from Mind, not from body.

I told this story to a group of visitors one day at Swannanoa. A man who had bought my book, *God Will Work With You But Not For You,* called to me as he was leaving, "It was worth the dollar I paid to come up here, for my wife to hear that story." Everyone joined good-humoredly in the laughter that followed his remark, for there are many who feel the way his wife did about making beds and the many other household chores.

One story always recalls another one. While writing the one about the beds, I recall the one about my beloved husband when he was mowing lawns. He was not the gardener type, but there was a period in his life when he had to mow lawns. He truly loved everything he did, and put joy into every task. That was why all of his great works in the arts, literature and science were masterly and beautiful.

When he mowed the lawns, he made patterns to mow, and in this way a routine job became interesting. No man I have ever known expressed the great joy he did in *everything* that he did. There was never anything that was too much trouble for him to do. If ever some little thing was broken, he would say, *"I'll fix it, darling."* He would leave more important work to do some odd little "fixing" job—and always with a smile of joy to be helping. And when someone else did something to help me, he would say, *"I bless anyone who does anything to help my Lao."*

TRUE LOVE IS FOREVER

It is the *little* things we all treasure about a person. The big things we take in our stride, but the simple, homely little things we remember forever. It truly is the everyday living and sharing that counts. We do not break a marriage with one we feel *comfortable* with. A marriage is really not a marriage at all when people are strangers after years of being together. We all know people like this. They *live* together, but they are still strangers because they cannot share their innermost thoughts with each other. Their marriage may not fail in the sense we think of a failure in marriage, but actually it has never been a marriage in the real sense.

When a marriage breaks, it breaks because true love was not its basis in the beginning. Love—true love—never dies, for love is of the Soul and, therefore, eternal. *Wait for your true love and your marriage will last FOREVER.*

CHAPTER VI

The Secret of Holding Romance

The secret of holding romance lies in holding the interest of the loved one. And how does one hold that interest?

First, let us consider just what romance means. Life itself is a tremendous adventure, and mankind a miraculous Creation.

The most exciting and beautiful experience in life is finding that one who makes *you* feel whole because you feel a completeness with him or her. That special someone will surely satisfy the deep longing for oneness in your heart, and bring contentment to your everyday living.

It is always in the little things shared with love that we find our greatest happiness. Who has not longed for an open fire, beautiful music, a dog or cat on the hearth, a bird singing his songs of love to his mate, a favorite beverage, and some special tidbit. Simple pleasures, but truly the greatest pleasures of all.

MUTUAL INTERESTS

What teen-ager does not dream of dancing with the object of his or her love? And never forget, *inside* we all feel like teen-agers about romance. To share any interest together makes people *think* together, and thinking gives birth to everything we do, individually or collectively. To dance, swim, hike, paint, sculpt, visit art galleries, and, etc., together, is all part of romance. I remember a student of ours telling me about her visit to the Boston Art Museum. There was a picture there that fascinated her so much that she would periodically go to see it. One day, she sat gazing at this picture when a young man came and sat nearby. He, too, loved this particular picture and, since thoughts are things, they became aware of each other. They found themselves talking to each other about the picture. They discovered that they shared a liking for other treasured pictures in the museum, and it was the most natural thing in the world that they became better acquainted. They made that *most* important discovery—they found they *liked* each other. We can *never* keep a romance alive unless we *like* each other, which means we have mutual respect of and for each other. In the case of this young couple, their mutual love of art led to a beautiful romance and marriage.

The more things you can *do* together, the greater is the basic interest in each other. There *must* be admiration as well as love.

My beloved husband and I did every little and big thing together. We wrote, painted, sculptured, read, danced, listened to beautiful music, played cards, walked, swam together, and even did mundane things, like cleaning house, together. In fact, we shared every wondrous moment together, and knew the ecstasy of true love.

We never failed to tell each other a dozen times a day how much we loved each other. Right to the end of his life, he would look up at me, with that glorious light of love in his eyes, and say, *"My darling, you are so beautiful."* And then he would say, *"When you go out of the room, the light goes out, and when you come in, it goes on again."* I would tell him that he was the most wonderful man in the whole wide world. In those last heartbreaking days, we whispered our eternal love for each other. Whatever one knows about eternal *oneness*, the physical separation is *never* easy. However, when we are fulfilling the purpose for which we were born—and every man is born to fulfill a purpose, whether he is aware of it or not—we can continue to live with joy in our hearts. Some day we know we shall again experience the fulfillment of true love with that one with whom we know *ONENESS* forever.

If anyone asked me the keynote of our lives together, I would say *BEAUTY*. All of the wonderful things that come under the heading of Beauty were ours. First under the heading of Beauty comes Love. For me, the word "Love" makes me think of tenderness and understanding, and the sharing of every precious moment. Then comes Humility, which recalls gratitude and appreciation of little and big things alike—beautiful music which brought

103

ecstasy to our souls, and made of each moment the eternal *NOW;* painting together to express a moment we had shared in Nature's garden of beauty; sculpturing together to express the Great Messenger of Love; writing together to extend cosmic knowledge of the wonders of man and his universe; dancing together, and knowing the rapture of floating as one to melodies that live within one's heart forever.

All these memories of moments shared were— and always will be—a fountain of living beauty.

I deeply desire for you to know that perfection which I found in love. Anyone can have this perfection in love if he does not compromise.

In writing of my marriage, I do so only to express my innermost feelings and knowledge of *why* it was so perfect. We can only extend that which we truly *know,* as we can only *accept* that which we are *ready* to accept.

Deep within all of us is the desire for a perfect mate—which means perfect love. The living of life is one long preparation for the ultimate experience of *LOVE*—not love as man has thought of love, but love as the Source and Power and the Eternal *all* of Life.

The ultimate *awareness* of *love* has to be earned. In my beloved husband's beautiful writings of *The Divine Iliad* are these meaningful words: *"All men will come to Me in due time but theirs is the agony of awaiting."* This means that we can do anything that we want to do, but we pay in agony of mind and in body the debt for all we do that does not fulfill Nature's Law of Balance.

THE AGONY OF UNBALANCE

I am going to quote briefly on **The Agony of Unbalance** from our year's *Home Study Course in Universal Law, Natural Science and Living Philosophy.*

"Life itself is a transcendent adventure. At its best, it is a tremendous adventure. At its best, it is tremendously difficult. It is a huge mountain of unknown height whose top is hidden in an impenetrable veil which every man must climb. From that upward journey of life, there is no escape for anyone, and no man knows what he must face on that lifelong climb up its tortuous paths of blazed and unmarked paths which he must tread in light or dark —and in the dark oft lose his way and pitch headlong into stark tragedy which may be his the very next moment after happiness and glory would seem to have been forever attained.

There are wonderful green meadows and forested paths on every man's mountain. There are babbling brooks and springs to quench his thirst— and fruit-laden trees and luscious gardens—and there is music of the singing of birds in the forests— and laughter and joy—and grief and death next door—and just beyond where a bride is lifted across her happy threshold a blind man gropes in the dark and a once proud scholar meets misery face to face and knows not what to do with it.

105

Love

Knows not what to do with it. . . . Therein lies the tragedy of life—the pitiful fact—you know not what to do with it.

YOU must face the unforeseen on your mountain. You must face its dangers for its paths are not all smooth. You must surmount its steep cliffs and lose your way in the dark. You must face failure as well as success, loneliness and frustration—lack of husband, home, children, love, or loss of them in death—or tragedy—or from your own weakness— or from treachery of trusted friends—AND KNOW WHAT TO DO WITH IT.

Yes, that is the tragedy in not knowing! Man on his mountain of life, not knowing his mountain—not knowing what to do when a wall of the mountain faces him—not knowing how to surmount it—having no compass to guide him—no Light of knowing out there in the dark of not knowing.

Woman on the mountain, terribly alone, frustrated and alone—not knowing what to do with it.

Boy on his mountain, homeless, penniless, helpless—for he knows not what to do with it.

But we know a man who has not been able to move for thirty years—blind—paralyzed—speech and hearing alone left to him—yet radiantly happy —successful—known, loved and honored—paying his way and giving much to the world—for he knows what to do with it.

We know hundreds of men and women who have

106

faced insurmountable hurdles and knew what to do with them. We have faced many of them ourselves and knew exactly what to do with them. And, doubtless, you have also.

Why such despair? Why such misery? Why fear anything in all this glorious universe of God's making and your making—where naught but life is— where you KNOW that you are existent as you in all creating things and cannot be alone, nor unhappy, nor defeated, nor in any way stopped from your joyful climb up your mountain of life to the Light of KNOWING which will illumine your path all of its glorious way if you but know what to do with life as you meet it ever in the Light in which there is no dark.

KNOWLEDGE ALONE CONTROLS YOUR DESTINY

Knowledge alone will help us meet our problems squarely and turn those which are seemingly not good into good—or those which seemingly hurt us into helpful ones which glorify us.

Everything which happens to us is good. Knowledge of our balanced universe will tell us that if all of our ills arise from unbalance, and our universe cannot be unbalanced, then we can balance our ills with that knowledge. Until we do balance them, they are but experiences which are our lessons in life.

107

*Until we do balance them we must regard them as
but stepping-stones across the stream of life."*

The application of the inviolate Law of Balance
will bring you balance—which means happiness—in
any and *all* of your transactions and interchanges.
Applying this law to sex interchange, we shall find a
"forever" romance as the net result. Balance is an
explanatory word for LOVE. Think of it in and
through this simple example. If a boy takes a girl in
sex whom he does not truly love, he is violating the
Law of Balance. He will surely make her unhappy as
he, himself, will be unhappy. By the same token, if a
girl gives herself to a boy whom she does not love,
she will make him unhappy as well as herself. There
is not anything that can separate two people who
fulfill the law of Rhythmic Balanced Interchange.
Neither is there anything that can keep two people
happily together but a fulfillment of the Law of Love
(*BALANCE*).

When we are young we often resent advice. And
even when we seek it—at any age—we seldom take
it. We go on our own blundering way, and have to
take the consequences of our mistakes. *Actually we
are the only ones who can take care of our own
problems, for we are the only ones who bring them
into being.* No matter what our problems may be, we
are the only ones who know their *cause.* Even *we*
may forget all of the issues that gave birth to
them.

THE GREAT NEED FOR SEX KNOWLEDGE

Sex problems are the root cause of countless other problems. That is why there is a necessity for scientific knowledge on this all-important factor in our lives.

When people have perfect and balanced sex lives, they approach other life problems with far greater tolerance and understanding than those who do not have sex-balance.

Sex problems are the net result of our sex practices. Not only are our bodies affected by sex, but our thinking is also influenced.

In my husband's book, *Scientific Answer to Sex Promiscuity*, he says, *"Each individual Self is the sum total of all of his sex decisions. Each person is what he is because of his sex decisions. To insulate one's Self from all unfavorable sex unions, voluntary, involuntary, social and sexual, and to contact that which will build a Self into a greater Self, is the supreme achievement of each moment of each life. . . . Nothing in life aids decadence so effectively as wrong mating and promiscuity, for each person either ascends or descends in body pattern to the level of the mate he chooses."*

My husband stressed the need for sex science when he said: *"As sex is the most important thing in shaping man's life—individually and collectively— sex science should be the most important fundamen-*

tal of his education, and dealt with as frankly as history or mathematics."

If the science of sex were more generally discussed, rather than the moral issue, young and old alike would understand the great importance of mate choosing. Our divorce rate proves this point. Because of moral censure and economic reasons, many couples stayed together in the past. Our present age does not so seriously consider these reasons.

THE GREAT IMPORTANCE OF BALANCED MATING

Everyone should know the importance of *balanced mating*. A marriage which is based purely upon physical attraction is not a balanced mating. *There must be a spiritual, mental, and physical harmony to fulfill the electrical balance necessary for balanced matehood.*

There is no law on earth that will hold two people together who do not truly love each other. They may live under the same roof, but this does not mean oneness in love and a true marriage. Every living creature desires romance, for this is the stimulus of all life. If you watch a little male bird, you will see him primping up before his chosen "lady" friend. He will pirouette around and around to attract her attention, sing her sweet melodies, and never give up until he does gain her attention. If anyone thinks that *any* little male bird will mate with *any* little female bird, he should put one of each sex in a cage together. Unless there is a very definite attraction between the birds, there will be hostility and what we call "hen pecking" taking place. I know because I witnessed this with parakeets. *Two mismated birds —or any form of life—will ultimately destroy the other if they are forced to stay together.*

On the other hand, each day I watch our little male and female wild birds. I have had a feeder outside of my window for years, and we have the same families of cardinals, wrens, titmice, sparrows, and various other birds, coming to feed all year round. To watch the "married" couples is pure joy. The little females often lift their heads and open their mouths for the males to drop in seeds they have peeled for them. One can *feel* their love of each other and can see the same mates coming and eating year after year.

I have observed that birds have a very definite code of ethics. You will see them giving each other an opportunity to use the feeder, regardless of species. It appears they all have a time limit, for I have noticed that newcomers will hover close by until those feeding have had their allotted time. If the ones feeding, however, stay too long, the newcomers will come and perch on the feeder until those eating fly away.

Man can learn so much from the habits of wildlife. There are very few animals, for instance, who do not give loving attention to their young in the days following the birth of their babies. Then they

111

teach them how to take care of themselves in the big wide world. Their discipline is often severe until they take heed.

The matter of discipline is also a forerunner of happy matehood later. An undisciplined child all too often grows into a selfish, self-centered human being who is unmindful of others' feelings. Such thoughtless people do not make good husbands or wives.

Love is a self*less* quality of Being. It knows none of the negative qualities of selfishness, envy, or jealousy. The negative qualities are the destructive qualities which have no part in the living of love.

The true secret of holding romance, is to *be* love by living the qualities of love. *We die within if we do not live love; man's very purpose on earth is to become in tune with all life and live joyously. Our lifelong search could be put into one word—ROMANCE.*

CHAPTER VII

True Love

"True love, true love; I give to you and you give to me, true love, true love . . ." Who does not love to hear that song, and hear it sung by a soft caressing voice! My beloved and I used to sit hand in hand while listening to this song, which all who are in love take delight in hearing.

And *I Love You Truly*, will ever be a favorite, not only for weddings, but for everyone in love.

When bad news is broadcast and then you hear a love song directly afterwards, it has a healing effect upon your heart. It is like the warmth of sunshine after rain caressing your cheeks with love after tears.

O! life that holds not love—it is not life at all. All life seems empty and pointless.

Therein lies your problem—and all men's problems when they know not what to do because they know not Love.

That is why you—and every other "you"—*must* know, as that other beautiful song says, *You Never Walk Alone*. You *must* know the Source of your very Self is Love.

That really *is* TRUE LOVE—and *it is forever-*

more. If I did not *know* this now I, too, would desire to refold.

God said to me on my high mountain-top, *"You shall know space but never emptiness."* And from that moment on, I knew Love—True Love—and never since that time have I known a moment's *emptiness,* the awful, terrifying emptiness.

When you know that Universal Love *within* you, you know all Love. It is then you are *ready* for love and that personal love you have always desired will come to you. This is why you must know your Self. The real wonder of *you* lies *within* you. Find that *YOU*—the real you—and you *will* know Love *forevermore*.

That great personal love will come to you, if necessary, from the other end of the world. One day, when you *least* expect it, the door will open, and he or she will walk into your life.

You remember the lovely song, "Some enchanted evening . . . You will see her . . .—You will see him . . ."

I can tell you this with all the conviction in my Soul, for that is what happened to me. And now, even though the body of my beloved has refolded, I shall have his love *forevermore*.

That is what True Love always is—*FOREVERMORE*.

Love forevermore—yes—this is the promise of The Universal One who created us. *Free will gave us the right to earn this LOVE*—ours to have and to hold forever—or to wander through life a stranger to all that brings *eternal* joy.

OUR ETERNAL SEARCH FOR LOVE

Your search for Love begins the moment you are born. Therefore, it is important you learn the *cause* of all things—then you will learn to know the difference between that which is *Cause* and that which is *Effect.*

All through the previous pages of this book I have tried to show the *Cause* and *Effect* of *Love,* and how *Balance* is the key to sustained love and happiness.

Understanding *love* as being *cause,* you will recognize that affection and sex are but the *effects* of love. Love is a spiritual, *mental* quality, and sex is a *physical effect.* Affection is also an effect of love.

The true and basic meaning of the love we seek is *balance.* If there is balance in your romancing—as I have explained in various instances—there will be sustained love; and, if there is love, there will be peace and ecstasy within you. No incident from henceforth will leave you with that deadening feeling of emptiness. The vacuum will *always* be filled with a sense of *security.*

Perhaps momentarily you will become disturbed over some trifling incident, and some big incident will seem like a mountain of trouble, but it will quickly pass. Not *anything* can disturb that inner lake of tranquility when you know Love—True Love.

115

HOW TO *FIND* THAT PERFECT LOVE

And how can you find that perfect love? O! that is the big question. That true love you have longed for from birth has to be *earned*. *That is the whole purpose of your whole life*—learning *the way* you can earn it.

Every experience you have has a deep purpose and, as I explained to you previously, of primary importance is what you gain in *inner* unfolding of character from those incidents.

Never forget that all and everything that happens in life came into being through *cause* and is, therefore, *purposeful*. Life itself is the most "purposeful" thing in the universe. *It is not just to earn money, to eat three meals a day, wear fine clothes, own and drive a car, seek and have sex, and all the other daily physical things we do to sustain and entertain our bodies, then go to bed to rest so that we can get up in the morning for a repeat performance.*

The very *purpose* of your being on earth, as a living, breathing entity, is so that you will make that unparalleled discovery of what Life and Love truly are. It is because the discovery of *what* Life and Love are is so *simple* that man has *not* discovered his purpose for being. He has made life complicated and purpose*less* and, until he discovers the *real secret of life,* he will continue to create his many problems, tragedies, and agonies.

116

UNDERSTANDING WHAT MOTIVATES YOU

YOU—and all mankind—are gradually becoming aware of *WHO YOU ARE—WHAT YOU ARE*—and *WHAT YOUR PURPOSE ON EARTH REALLY IS*. When you comprehend and put into practice the Natural Laws which motivate you, you will not have sex problems. Neither will the many other problems, which now beset so many human beings, unbalance their thinking to the point where they do not desire to live. With understanding, one strives to *live* the laws of Nature which must be adhered to in order that Balance be maintained in all of our interchangings, whether physical, mental, or spiritual.

When you find true love, it becomes the motivating force of your life. There is an old saying, *"Love of man's life is but a part; it is woman's whole existence."* I do not believe this statement applies to the man who truly loves. I know that men need—and seek—true love as much as women; for they, too, are only half of the balanced life principle without their mates. It does, however, bring to mind the story of "BAMBI." This sensitive story, written by Felix Salten, beautifully portrays the feelings of the little doe, Bambi, and that of her mate. You may have seen the wonderful movie Walt Disney made of this story.

Bambi, heavy with her young, sadly watched her

mate disappear over the horizon to seek new adventure. As you read the author's sensitive understanding of her longing to join him, you know she is baffled at his leaving her alone.

This story shows that all life wonders at the WHY and difference of male-female attitudes. There is only *one* solution to this heartache that either a woman or man experiences during the gamut of years. It is a lesson that *is* hard to learn and it sometimes takes many unhappy experiences to learn it. The solution lies in being completely happy *within* yourself. We are happy within ourselves when we cease to think of ourselves *first*. It is in loving service to others that we unfold within. The reason for this is because we are fulfilling Nature's law of love in *giving*.

THE SPIRIT OF CHRISTMAS

For a few days each year, there is a spirit of giving with love that pervades the air. That period is Christmas time. Christmas Love is the Light of God's Love expressed by GIVING love.

That deep pleasure we know at Christmas does not come to us when we are *receiving* gifts; it comes when we *give* gifts. And it is not the gift itself which really touches someone's heart; it is the *thought* behind the gift. When we give, we are fulfilling the first law of Nature, which is to give, and that is why we are filled with a sense of ecstasy.

Many people feel that they have to prove their

love by buying an expensive gift, and often they do not give a gift at all because they have not the means for what they feel is a suitable gift for a certain person or family.

They are so far from the truth in this. We had a friend who was very wealthy, and each year it was quite a challenge to find him some little gift he could use. I would hunt and hunt for that "something" I felt would please him. One year, I found a tiny traveling air mail scales that folded up in a little leather case. This man was like most other very wealthy people, extremely careful with his pennies and hated to put an extra stamp on a letter when not sure of the weight. He was delighted with this gift, and I was more delighted than he because I had found that little "something" that he could use and be really pleased with.

This man once confided to me that because people knew he was wealthy, they never seemed to realize that a little gift would give him great pleasure. It was not that he wanted gifts of "things" as much as to know someone cared enough to hunt for something for him. I knew he treasured our friendship because I did remember his birthday and Christmas.

Realizing the depth of our happiness in giving at Christmas time, we can make *every* day of our lives Christmas Day by giving of ourselves lovingly in some service to each other.

Never fail to show appreciation. It is not *thanks* we want so much as appreciation. You know how *you* feel inside when you see that look of joy spreading over someone's face when you give him a gift. That joy is *reflected* in you. It multiplies itself in you and touches everything in the universe. When *you* tremble with happiness, the whole world vibrates with your happiness. The saying, *"Laugh and the world laughs with you,"* is truer than man knows.

Would it not be wonderful if we had the spirit of Christmas giving in everything we do? The measure of love you give is *unfailingly* the measure of love you will be *regiven*.

I never hear that phrase about making every day Christmas Day, that I do not recall a statement made by a precious little girl. Her parents were preparing for a drive in the country, and she said, *"Let us go to Swannanoa. Every day is Christmas Day at Swannanoa."*

Children are always aware of our moods. Surface appearances do not fool them.

All dog lovers will tell you that this is true with dogs, also. People who love and understand dogs do so because a dog's love is the kind of love every human being would like to find in his fellow man. He loves you whether you live in a hut or a palace. He loves you for YOU, not for what you give him or for what you look like. If you are early or late coming to him, he wags his tail joyously, and you know beyond any doubt that he *wants* to be with you sharing your joys and your sorrows. He does not care whether your skin is white, red, yellow, brown, or black. To

120

him you are supreme. He just *loves* you. And then men say of some debauched human being, *"He is lower than an animal."* If only all mankind could be as loving and forgiving as a faithful dog!

Animals are guided by what man calls instinct (Natural Law). It is a rare animal of any species that kills more than it can eat in one day, which he needs to survive. Man, who lives mainly according to *Man Law,* has reached that high stage, technologically, where he kills by the million. Which, therefore, can be called "higher than" or "lower than"?

WHAT IS TRUE LOVE?

True love is perfect Balance, both within one's self and extended to one's fellow man, whether that fellow man is one's sweetheart, husband, wife, father, mother, child, friend, or business associate.

Until a person "finds" himself, and is truly happy within himself, he cannot be happy with anyone. It was Polonius in Shakespeare's *Hamlet* who said: *"This above all: to thine own self be true, and it follows, as the night the day, thou canst not then be false to any man."*

Philosophers through the ages have told man this same truth, but man has not understood the great importance of this statement. It has, therefore, remained an abstract statement instead of becoming a vital living philosophy.

True love is placing the loved one *before* one's self. When you truly love, you do this naturally and

121

automatically. You think *first* of the loved one. By so doing, you are fulfilling the *first* great law of the universe which is GIVING. The *only* thing that Life can *give* to us is that which *we first give to it*. This is the greatest—and most difficult—lesson of Life. *Learn it, and you will hold the key to Romance, Success, Health, Wealth, and Happiness.*

Everyone *can give first* even though it is some small thing that he cherishes. As a child, if someone had a birthday, and I did not have money to buy a gift, I would give him one of my favorite possessions. I would always save all of my pennies, which were given to me for pocket money, and buy little gifts. My mother would be quite distressed because I would not spend my pocket money on myself. When we went for a holiday, I would want to go and buy gifts with my savings the very first day of our arrival. The fact we would not be going home for two weeks, sometimes, would not stop me from wanting to get the gifts right away.

I was not aware, at the time, that this strong desire to give was a fulfillment of the first law of the universe; but, all of my life, there has been a great regiving to me, and my cup has been full to overflowing with love and all the things that make life beautiful. That is why it is important that everyone understands the law of giving and regiving. As we are only truly happy when we are creating and accomplishing, so are we only truly happy when we are *giving*.

It has been through man's unawareness of this basic law of *giving* that he has failed to find the key to *love, unity, and peace on earth.* Man may say that he knows this great law—but if he truly *knew* this inviolate law he would *live* it. He has endorsed the law of giving, as he has endorsed the law of love, but he has not lived these laws. Those who do know and live them have been outnumbered by the all too many who have not lived them—perhaps unknowingly. The state of our world today bears witness to this fact.

TRUE LOVE

How will you *know* when you have found true love? You will not need to ask that question when you find it; you will know beyond a doubt that it is yours forever. It will flow from you to everyone, for you will become as a fountain of living water from which others will come to quench their thirst.

Every man and woman desires true love. True love is the expression of balanced matehood, and this grows out of deep respect, one for the other. The application of the Law of Balance to two lives united in love could not fail to bring success to that greatest and most beautiful experience of our lives—MARRIAGE.

So let our hearts sing, *"True love, true love; I give to you and you give to me, Love FOREVERMORE."*

Walking with her pet Scotty on a sparkling, snowy day is one of the author's greatest joys. Beautiful Swannanoa Palace, headquarters of the University of Science and Philosophy, is seen in the background.

Lovingly,
Lao Russell

The author before the Italian Cararra marble fireplace in the baronial hall at Swannanoa. On the mantel can be seen the four priests from the trial of Joan of Arc. Walter Russell's sculptural masterpiece of "The Mark Twain Memorial" represents characters from four of Mark Twain's favorite books.

The author standing beside her late husband's famous painting, "The Might of Ages," which symbolizes the power of accumulative thought in the building of a civilization. This painting has received highest awards and honors from eleven foreign countries. Walter Russell's sculptured bust of the renowned musician, Leopold Godowsky, is seen in the background.

The author with her late husband's beautiful sketch model of "The Four Freedoms." His portrait of Hudson Maxim can be seen at the author's right.

The author standing beside a self-portrait bust of her late husband. Shown also in the picture is Dr. Russell's portrait of Bishop Alexander Garrett and his bust of conductor-composer Ossip Gabrilowitsch.

The author showing students Walter Russell's sculpture of Mark Twain and Tom Sawyer. These are the central figures of his "Mark Twain Memorial." The glass-topped table in the foreground contains historic photographs and documents of the author's and her late husband's life.

The author is proud of her late husband's woodcarving. This chair was in constant use in their studio in Carnegie Hall, New York. It is one of his many wood carvings now on exhibition at Swannanoa.

Lao Russell returning from a walk with her little Scotty, Wendy.

Part II

"When the world of man serves the world of man with love, the peace which passeth all understanding will then come to him."
—From *The One-World Purpose,*
by LAO and WALTER RUSSELL

CHAPTER VIII

The Vital Role of Today's Youth

Youth has the most vital role to play in this crucial period of mankind's unfolding. A new era is in the birth throes. In giving birth to anything there is usually pain. However, there follows the triumph of overcoming. This critical history-making period is no exception to the rule. This is a time of trial, error, and *effort. You,* who are teen-agers today with the enthusiasm of youth, can bring into being an unparalleled period in history for, technologically, man has reached unparalleled heights. He now needs—and *must* have—the balance of CHARACTER. *You can make tomorrow triumphant by what you do today.*

Let us see *how* you can help create a happy, balanced world. Since sex is the great motivating force of all life, let us first consider the *unbalanced* emphasis on sex in our lives today.

MAN'S SELF-CREATED TENSIONS

Before the fall of every great civilization, there is an emphasis on sex, which is caused by frustrating

135

tensions. People not knowing the *cause* of these tensions turn to sex for release. The tragedy for them is that, instead of finding release, they build more and greater tensions. *Sex without love feeds but half of man's sex hunger, and multiplies his tensions accordingly.*

All excesses are self-destructive. Excessive and promiscuous sex lead to self-condemnation and often to *suicide*. Excessive drinking and smoking can lead to narcotics which will destroy man morally and physically.

The tensions which exist in your home, and in almost every other home in the world today, are causing conditions which are hard for many people to understand. These tensions create frustrations in young and old alike.

THE SOLUTION LIES IN KNOWING *CAUSE*

The multiplication of today's tensions is leading to world-suicide at an ever-increasing rate, and there is but *one* solution. And what *is* the solution? The *solution lies in the reversal of man's thinking, which influences his human behavior and gives birth to every incident on earth.* Man now thinks primarily through his *senses* instead of through his *Mind*. In thinking through his senses, he desires only to satisfy his senses. He finds he not only does *not* satisfy his physical urges, but he hates himself. *Self-hate multiplies itself into world-hate.*

136

The Vital Role of Today's Youth

The one and only solution lies in man's "discovering" himself. When he at last comprehends his true oneness—or relationship—with every other man, he will begin to live the great and inviolate Law of Love. That day *must come soon* otherwise it will be too late to stem the tide that can envelop the whole world.

Therefore, it is obvious we need basic knowledge of *what* motivates mankind. Unless we know the *how* and *why* of things, we do not know the *cause*. Not knowing the *cause* we cannot find the solution.

Youth is rebelling against present conditions and clamoring to know the *cause*—not truly knowing *why* it is rebelling. There is a need to go *beyond information* and understand *cause* through *inner knowledge. We have an abundance of information to remember and repeat but knowledge, which gives birth to idea, is not encouraged.*

Youth wants basic knowledge which will satisfy its idealism and give it the truth—not a clouded truth in meaningless words but a truth that can be dynamically proven scientifically.

Young people are questioning, as well they might, *why* we have one war after another and uneasy *truces* between wars to settle men's differences. They do not see our world growing better after each war; they see it getting worse. *We are not living in a happy and peaceful world when half the world is at war, or hungry, or imprisoned, or dying.*

137

Every day we see and hear stories of divorces, crime, war, suicide, and other tragedies, which greatly add to our personal fears and tensions. It is small wonder that youth is confused.

The root *cause* of all man's problems lies in his ignorance of *who he is—what he is—and what his purpose on earth is.* Scientific knowledge is available which can answer all of these vital questions, and bring a solution to our many personal and world problems.

IN TRUTH IS FREEDOM

The following letter is from a wonderful young man who came to some of my lectures this spring. He is one of you, and a legion of such young men will eventually give birth to a world united in Truth.

"Dear Lao,

I had to write you a letter of thanks for the impression you made on me in two of your recent lectures in southern California.

Probably you don't remember me, but I remember you and your angelic composure and your traveling tea service of fine china. I even remember your nephew Peter in England, whom you mentioned when you autographed your book God Will Work <u>With</u> You But Not <u>For</u> You.

I'm now in the service of my country, and service has a newer meaning in my life. It's the type of service to a higher truth which I saw radiating from your face as you "conversed" with those audiences in California. I haven't once felt homesick since I left home, but not because I haven't fond recollections of home. Rather, I acknowledge that home is where my Father is and there is nowhere else I can be. A beautiful memory I have is saying goodbye at the airport. My mother and father were smiling and I was happy, too. It was a moment of supreme faith in that higher Truth: the same faith you had when you spoke.

That's all I had to say: just thank you for standing in front of me and saying, 'This is what happens when you follow the instructions in the books.' I've read the books all my life. They are very pretty like poetry, but the books really mean something when the teacher is there, and you see what happens and what life can mean to the individual. This letter is probably as clear as mud, but I had to write it. I look forward to four years in the Air Force applying myself to the maintenance of peace.

Yours very sincerely,

P. C. A."

As I read this cherished letter, the words of a World War I veteran came to mind. He was one of a group from a Veterans Hospital who had been brought to Swannanoa to hear one of my talks. He was in full accord with my remarks about knowing the power of God within, and he said, *"You are so right. I remember that when we went 'over there' the* ones who said they would come back, did come back. The one's who thought they would not, didn't."

He showed me a long scar on his arm, saying, *"All I got was this, but I did come back."*

Truth is freedom because, when it becomes a part of our thinking, our fears are voided.

THE LAW OF BALANCE IN ACTION

Your vital role is to know yourself, to live without compromise, and to fulfill your purpose on earth. You can do this by putting into practice Nature's Laws and her ways and processes.

The world is out of balance because man has unbalanced human relations. *Every unbalanced condition has been created by man.* Nature always balances herself if we give her the chance—and time.

Man may cause a temporary unbalance in Nature by his thoughtless destruction. However, man's life span is brief. Nature, on the other hand, has millions of years, if necessary, to restore the destruction wrought by man. For instance, witness how man has taken from Mother Earth and made her barren of trees to the point of destroying our very planet through his unbalanced taking.

Man cannot have water without an abundance of trees, and yet men for centuries have bankrupted *themselves* of the one thing they cannot survive without—water.

140

Richard St. Barbe Baker, one of the world's foremost foresters told me, *"If a man loses a third of his skin, he dies, if a tree loses a third of its bark it dies, and if the world loses a third of its trees it will die."* This man of Nature has a great plan to reclaim the Sahara Desert, the reforestation of which would give food and land for millions of people.

Man also bankrupts the earth by not putting back into it what he takes from it. In the old days, we carefully saved all of our leaves in the autumn, and made compost heaps of them; today we burn them, and lose lifegiving minerals. This is but one of the many ways that man takes from the earth, and does not regive.

COUNTRY LIFE

One who loves country life always feels sorry for those who have not discovered the exciting and beautiful world of Nature. No one can ever be lonely as he walks in the woods and discovers the pulsing, singing, courageous, growing trees, and the bright, glowing beauty of wild flowers—an endless array of them. Each month you discover another species. Did you know that there are actually about twenty-five kinds of chickweeds? Their little white flowers contain tiny capsules of small seeds that songbirds love.

Nature is far more exciting than odor-filled cities whose streets are filled with raucous noises, instead of the sound of the songs of birds, the rustle of leaves,

141

falling twigs, and the "chatter" of wildlife both far and near.

More young people should study Natural Law. If they did, many more would become fascinated with Mother Earth and desire to "go back to the farm." We would not have a shortage of farm help if young people realized the wonder and beauty of growing things. No life is as exciting as forest life, and yet man crowds into cities where there is tension created by man who all too often desires to build transitory wealth for his body, instead of permanent wealth for his Soul.

My beloved was living in New York when we met, and I said to him, *"I have but one request to make— when we are married we must live in the country. I am a country girl at heart, and it would lengthen your life by years."* He was seventy-four years old when we met, and he lived to be ninety-two. It did prolong his dear life by many years. He, of course, adored the country for he, too, deeply loved Nature.

This does not mean we do not love and appreciate the many wonderful privileges a great city or town has to offer. We loved the great concerts, opera, good shows, and dining and dancing in a luxurious restaurant. It is lots of fun occasionally. All of the exciting things a big city has to offer are far more exciting when it is an "occasion." *Balance* of both the town and country is again the answer and key to contentment. It is through this very balance in our way of life that we make life itself a grand and glorious adventure. It is all up to us.

BALANCED GIVING—UNBALANCED TAKING

Not anything comes into being in our human interchangings without our bringing it into being. Man has free will to bring Love or Hate into being. *Love is born of balanced givings. Hate is born from unbalanced takings.* The choice is *always* ours.

A Message of Love was given to the world two thousand years ago. *Man endorsed that message of love, but how many men have truly lived it?*

Other inspired messages of Love and Wisdom have been given, but man has not heeded them by living them. *The reason he has not lived them, is because he has been blinded by body sensation and desire for material possessions.* When he learns to possess possessions, instead of possessions possessing him, he will begin to seek the invisible qualities which give permanent joy.

The time has now arrived when many realize that physical sensation does not satisfy, and material possessions are as nothing if we do not have the love and cooperation of our fellow man.

We now have the choice of *living* the great Law of Love—which means *BALANCE*—in all of our interchangings, or we shall destroy the planet, itself, through ignorance and greed which are a violation of Nature's Law of Balance.

That is WHY your role today is of such vital importance. *You can put the Law of Balance into operation by living it.*

143

THE LAW OF CAUSE AND EFFECT

When man comprehends the Law of Cause and Effect, and that CAUSE is the desire-energy within Mind to manifest Mind-Idea, he will begin to put into practice higher knowledge of sex, and know the ecstasy and balance of mental harmony as well as physical sensation.

He can never progress toward happiness, peace, and prosperity, while he is physically dominated and limited to sensed-effect. World history shows that an increase in material power of expression, unbalanced by spiritual power, is always accompanied by a multiplication of crime, wars, and immorality, with an increase in sex and cultural degeneracy. War, itself, is the *effect* of fear.

We are all *aware* of the tensions and hate in our world today. However, *our greatest hope lies in that very awareness.* Our worldwide conditions are proof that the time is *here* when we must throw away our old pagan ways of killing, and put into practice that one inviolate law of the universe—*Rhythmic Balanced Interchange*—which is based upon the love principle of giving for regiving, or perish from this earth. Man truly has no other choice, for he is now in his midnight hour *and knows it.*

THE INVIOLATE LAW OF RHYTHMIC BALANCED INTERCHANGE

It was my late beloved husband, Dr. Walter Russell, who first gave the great law of *Rhythmic*

144

Balanced Interchange to the world. He explained this scientifically in his book entitled, *The Universal One,* which was published in 1926. In order that you may better comprehend this basic Law of Balance in its relation to our Human Relations, I will exemplify this in the following excerpt from our book entitled, *Scientific Answer to Human Relations.*

THE BASIC ROOT OF A BALANCED CIVILIZATION

"The very foundation of life lies in the desire of every man to give service to fulfill the needs of his neighbor.

The very essence of glorious living lies in this principle—so you must fully understand it. You wonder why we do not complete the above paragraph by adding these words: "so that his neighbor will give service to him to fulfill his needs."

If we added these words, we would be adding a motive for the giving of love—a selfish motive. There is no selfish motive in Nature. There is no need for it. That, also, is law, for law itself compels an equal reaction to every action. Nature is a creation of love. There is no selfishness in love. Desire to give must be without motive other than desire to give.

Heaven does not give to earth because it desires gifts from earth. It gives solely because it has been given in abundance of itself and must give out from itself that which has been given to it to regive.

Likewise, earth does not give its forests to the heavens because it expects gifts of rains in payment thereof. Earth gives solely because it has been given an abundance of itself which it must give out to manifest itself—even as the composer genius must give out music without thought of compensation for he would thus manifest himself if he were alone in the wilderness.

There is naught in this creating universe which gives aught than the over-abundance of itself which has first been given it. The sun gives of its light without motive other than giving of itself. God's one law of balanced interchange regives to the sun that which has been given by the sun, just as forests given by earth to heavens to manifest earth are regiven by heavens to earth to manifest heavens.

THE UNLEARNED LESSONS OF MAN

The great lesson to learn of life is the need of giving out from the abundance of one's self in order to be ever abundant within one's self.

Every man is a fount of living waters which must ever flow to keep them ever living. He who shuts off the fountains of his abundant self stagnates the living waters of his living self and contaminates all things with his very breathing.

He who withholds his giving deprives himself alone of the gifts of his desiring.

Where earth withholds for itself that which it

The Vital Role of Today's Youth

should give, its founts dry up and parched deserts tell of the withholding.

When man withholds that which he should give out of himself to enrich himself he, instead, subtracts from the abundance of himself in the measure of his withholdings.

He who withholds love from his home—or from his neighbor—makes a desert for his very soul. And he who gives love to receive love will find in his receiving the taint which was in his giving.

He who serves abundantly will be served with abundance, yea, and he who gives more of service than has been asked of him will multiply within himself that which he has over-given by increasing his capacity for giving. Love cannot be possessed; therefore, ask not for love but give it.

The carpenter, or mason, or butcher and all who serve, who limit the service they give to less than that which they receive—thinking that they are thereby enriched—are instead impoverished with a poverty which multiplies within them as microbes of destruction multiply their power to destroy that within which they grow.

Cross not the sacred threshold of your neighbor's house without love in your heart. And when you recross that threshold into the world, carry naught but love there also, for he who carries naught but love is loved by man, but he who carries aught but love is despised by those whose love he most needs.

147

NATURE NEVER BARGAINS. NATURE BALANCES

The suns of space and the earths which circle them dare not violate the law of Rhythmic Balanced Interchange. If our earth just dared for one day to change its orbit, all the seas of earth would strip it clean and wash man into its seas. Yet man dares to violate this law—and when disaster overtakes him, he wonders why such things happen to him. He recovers and does it again, and yet again. Man is slow to learn his greatest lesson.

Man has but one price with man for service interchange, and that price is equality in regivings for all who give. To him who gives little, little must be regiven but its value must be equal to the value of service given. And to him who gives much, much must be regiven. That is law. It is fixed and cannot be ignored.

He who takes more than his balanced share and pays less to the producers of his wealth fills chests with useless gold which both impoverishes him and all the world of men. The worker also consumes— but what can a consumer buy with an empty purse? And what does it profit a man whose shelves are piled high and no buyer enters his door?"

As YOU comprehend and live the Law of Balance, you will have the *key* to all the wonderful things Life has to give. You have free will to choose.

148

In Balance there is *abundance*—in unbalance there is *poverty*.

HIGHER SEX KNOWLEDGE

There are many fine young men and women in our world today who are anxious to understand their role in the scheme of things, and how they can bring into being a better era than we have ever known.

When higher sex knowledge is taught in schools, and given primary attention, we shall take a great step forward towards a civilization which is balanced and, therefore, stable.

There *is* a great transformation occurring in the human race in spite of the terrifying outside appearances. Mankind is painfully and slowly becoming transformed from purely sense-dominated man to Mind-knowing man.

The dissatisfaction men and women are experiencing in their various interchangings is not such a personal thing as it appears to be. It is rather a universal dissatisfaction. We become depressed when we cannot find a solution to our problems. The majority of people, today, do not know where to look for the solution for the many problems that are facing them individually as well as collectively.

Man knows, *within* himself, there *is* a solution to his problems; and he becomes irritated and tense when he knows not what to do with them. It is then he strikes out in all directions at those in his home circle, and at those in his work-a-day world.

149

Love

My husband wrote the following regarding the electrical nature of sex and its effects upon individuals—and the necessity of balanced sex relations—in his book, *Scientific Answer to Sex Promiscuity.*

"If youth can be instructed regarding the electrical nature of sex and its effects upon individual lives and progress, it would be a greater deterrent from promiscuity than merely <u>moral</u> or <u>physical</u> grounds. If young men and women are made aware that all the medical care in the world will not prevent their character deterioration if they disobey Natural Law, they will give more serious thought to man's greatest natural safeguard—marriage with a balancing mate."

The youth of today has a unique opportunity in that it could truly give birth to a unified and enduring civilization. There is an imperative necessity for balance in every transaction in life, and especially in the man-woman relationship.

We all know that over-indulgence in sexual relations does not bring lasting satisfaction, and we realize there is an ever-increasing degree of sex promiscuity.

What is the answer to this problem? The answer is obvious. *There must be a reversal of man's sexual practices*. This will come as man understands that it is not a *physical* balance he is seeking, as much as a Mind-awareness.

Self knowledge is of vital importance for everyone, since our purpose is to know the perfection of a balanced life. Our own lives must, therefore, become balanced in order that we can extend balance to our fellow man.

My husband further stated regarding higher intellectualism through balanced sex:

"This is a phase of knowledge which we are just beginning to comprehend and act upon in our building of higher intellectualism. It should be more fundamental in our educational system. Sex should not be judged as a moral issue, but as a biological and spiritual issue. It would be just as reasonable to judge explosions in chemical elements as immoral. Rather should we judge sex from the point of view of Natural Law and obey its demands in relation to mate choosing. The reason why practically everyone pays the high price of sex abuse is because sex is so little understood. Because of that ignorance, there is a rapid world decadence in culture at this very moment."

OUR NEW AGE

Every past age looks archaic to a new age. The youth of every age has called its elders "old-fashioned." In writing on this subject in our *Home Study Course,* we said:

"We, the human race, look about us and see how very enlightened we think we are. We have air travel, motor cars, television, radio and a thousand comforts unknown even one century ago, and admire ourselves as great people of a great age. We

151

look back upon those unenlightened people of yesterday and say they are old-fashioned people of the horse-and-buggy days. Those people of yesterday were ourselves. There were many great minds among them, many immortals who enriched this age.

We look back a thousand years—two thousand years—three thousand years. We now say that the civilization of their day was archaic. They thought this about the earth and that about the stars—and one tribe slaughtered another and took over its herds —and one king took away the lands of other kings. That was long ago, we say, when the earth was peopled with barbarians, but those people of that far yesterday were ourselves. There were many great minds among them, many immortals who enriched this age.

Shall we forget that tomorrow is not far away when people shall look upon us as archaic barbarians who had learned how to kill by millions instead of by ones? Will they judge our standards by the planes and motor cars of a material age of archaic reasoning in our science, disunity in our many religions, and parrot-like memorizing in our education?

What do you really think tomorrow will think of us? Can you really feel that we will be thought of as enlightened? Do you not feel that another age ahead would be justified in thinking of this age as being in its intellectual and spiritual infancy? You would undoubtedly resent this as men of Plato's age would resent your concept of their standards, but you will be one of tomorrow's age and you will undoubtedly think that way of us.

These people of tomorrow will be ourselves, yet there are many great minds of this age, many immortals of today who will have enriched mankind of tomorrow. And so it is that man forever seemingly unfolds without realizing that it is not man who unfolds but Mind-awareness which forever transforms man throughout the ages of Mind-manifestation through the body of man."

It seems of vital importance to include these thoughts from our teachings, because each day I read, hear, and witness, the confusion of young and old alike as to *what is wrong with our world today— and what can be done about it.*

COMPREHENDING OUR ONENESS

Thinking people know that a miracle cannot change the world conditions overnight. We know the frailties of human nature, and that, even though for a few brief hours people may suddenly be loving and kind, they very soon revert back to their old ways of grumbling, fighting, and hurting each other in diverse ways. Man does not change overnight. In fact, he changes very little in a lifetime. That is why he *creates* one war after another. As long as fear, crime, selfishness, and greed, and the wars which are their harvest, continue as the practices of men, just so

153

long will life be full of frustrations for the peace and happiness all people desire.

We gradually comprehend our oneness with each other as we share deeply inspiring experiences or major disasters. This *awareness* of our oneness is startlingly clear to us when some major catastrophe occurs like an earthquake, tornado, plane or car crash, etc. It may only be for a fleeting second but, when you hear the news, you experience the agony of your severance with people you have never known. Sometimes you actually sense their physical agony at their passing.

In my book, *God Will Work With You But Not For You,* I wrote of this experience in these words: *"You feel you have lost something of yourself. These moments of grief and distress are great moments of exaltation where love is all that is and all else ceases. These are your high moments when you are very close to God—and God is very close to you."*

I was talking to a woman today who was in a car accident. When she regained consciousness, she found that her husband, whom she adored, was lying dead, and her son badly injured. She, herself, was badly injured, but she said she experienced a sense of exaltation even through her great agony of mind and body. It was as though she, herself, were looking on from a distance. Many men wounded in war have experienced this temporary awareness of Mind. This temporary exaltation is because the body sensations

154

have been temporarily numbed through extreme shock and pain.

When President Kennedy was assassinated, millions of people knew their oneness with him, and felt the grief of his wife and family. This was one of the greatest universal sharings that we have ever known in our lifetime. No one felt a desire for gaiety. Cancellations for events like football games, movies, and parties, occurred not only all over this country but all over the world.

The expression of grief was not limited to and for President Kennedy and his family; it was something man felt deep within himself *for himself.* He, too, had been struck down, and he cried within himself for the security of Love—the kind of Love that can be ours *only* when we know our *oneness* with our Creator.

OUR INTERDEPENDENCE

We shall continue to create all of the conditions which now exist, until we give birth to a change of thinking through an ever-growing awareness of ourselves and our oneness and interdependence upon each other.

The most important element in building a civilization is the manner in which man deals with man.

The key to that awareness is *knowledge;* for ignorance, alone, keeps man imprisoned within his body, and compels that body ever to walk the tread-mill of a physical existence under the lash of its slavery.

YOU CAN GIVE BIRTH TO
AN AGE OF CHARACTER

There was a period, thousands of years ago, when Egyptians gave birth to a New Age of Character. In this period, there was a gradual unfolding of new thinking, and man found that in mutual interchange of service there were pleasurable feelings.

It would take many pages to write of the rise and fall of civilizations. The following is a brief excerpt from our *Home Study Course* regarding the birth of character and righteousness in man when the Age of Character began in Egypt:

"To understand man and to know what is the matter with man and man's world of today, it is necessary to go back to the very beginning of his awareness that he was more than sensed-man. That period was the Dawn of Consciousness, which means the very first awareness of his immortality. That was probably about eight thousand years ago, but two to three thousand years of twilight preceded that dawn of a sufficiently conscious awareness of morality, character and righteousness to form a social order where justice and a philosophy of life were strong enough to unify man's interests into what we call a civilization. During all of this period a language slowly grew, together with a way of writing that language in words and forms and sym-

bols. The Age of Character began in Egypt. Its rulers and its people considered character building as of first import. All else was secondary, as we shall see.

Then came into being an intellectual, moral, righteous, cultured and scientific civilization such as the world has never yet equaled in its spiritual standards, with the qualities which are essential to an enduring civilization. Man of the pre-Pyramid Age had never been surpassed as a moral intellectual during all of these thousands of years. The reason for that is because individual greed for physical possessions and power had not yet come into the world. People's desires were collective for the good of the whole. In man's discovery of man, he valued man above all things for he discovered that every man working together in unity could produce wonderful things.

Greed came gradually and did not gain force, to the detriment of character, until about the 25th century B.C. *From that time forward, man set the product of man before man himself. For this reason he has now become a part of his machine and is so considered. In appraising the value of any laborer, his ability to produce more output from his machine than another man is the measure of his worth. In the upper brackets of industry, the man who can produce more profit for his employer is the man of greater value. This has been the slow growth of centuries during which time man has forever*

157

thought of his civilization as highly advanced over the barbarous ages of the past.

Mankind still must learn that the most important thing in life is what one does to his neighbor."

This brief outline of this previous Age of Character is sufficient to indicate that only qualities of character can bring balance to our unbalanced world of today. Do we not all long to live in a world where man is happy to serve his fellow man, instead of trying to TAKE constantly from him? Do we not all desire to be loved for ourselves, alone, and not for what someone can get from us? Of course we do. We *all* want to be happy, and to be loved. It is an empty life, indeed, without someone who truly cares what happens to us.

YOUR DESIRES CREATE YOUR DESTINY

Every moment of your life you are molding your character, and it is your character that determines your destiny.

In my book, *God Will Work With You But Not For You,* are some thoughts on this as follows:

"Every man determines his own destiny by what he thinks and does every moment of his life. You can become what you want to be only through your thoughts and actions, but the measure of your desire must be great in order for you to become great. Hitch your wagon to a star and fasten its bolts with deep desire to manifest love and, behold, its wings will carry you to those heights.

158

The Vital Role of Today's Youth

No one who has ever reached those heights has done so by himself alone. He who loves is aware of Love working with him. . . . Love is the foundation of the universe. He who deeply loves is deeply humble. The greatest men in the world are those who are most humble. An arrogant man is one who asserts his personal ego, while the humble man is one who suppresses it and is, therefore, without arrogance. The quality of humility is that which gives to one the gentleness and tenderness of a spiritual strength which can best be described as saintly.

This universe of love is a universe of law, for love is law. He who works with the law of love is working with the universe, and the universe is working with him.

Every man who has ever become great became so only because he desired to, planned to, and made the effort to become so. There are no accidentally great men. All great men build themselves in their own image. That which they become, they first desired to become. They thought out and planned every step upward to their own high mountain-top. The great difference between all people lies not in their abilities but in the intensity of desire to express their abilities."

The following is a basic foundation for a living philosophy which I first released in my book *God Will Work With You But Not For You.*

CODE OF ETHICS

To bring blessings upon yourself bless your neighbor.

To enrich yourself enrich your neighbor.

Honor your neighbor and the world will honor you.

To sorely hurt yourself hurt your neighbor.

He who seeks love will find it by giving it.

The measure of a man's wealth is the measure of wealth he has given.

To enrich yourself with many friends enrich your friends with yourself.

That which you take away from any man the world will take away from you.

When you take the first step to give yourself to to that which you want, it will also take its first step to give itself to you.

Peace and happiness do not come to you from your horizon. They spread from you out to infinity beyond your horizon.

The whole universe is a mirror which reflects back to you that which you reflect into it.

Love is like unto the ascent of a mountain. It comes ever nearer to you as you go ever nearer to it.

THE DRAMA OF THE PLAY OF CREATION

In comprehending a little more clearly the nature of man and his inner motivating desire for Balance, you know that only man, himself, can bring fulfillment to his desire for peace on earth and good will towards all men.

You know the very *purpose* of the drama of the Play of Creation is that mankind learns from his experiences what to do, and what not to do, so that the *Law of Balance* is fulfilled.

The words of my husband which I gave you previously in this book, *"All men will come to Me in due time but theirs is the agony of awaiting,"* are wrought with deep meaning.

THE AGONY OF MAN'S AWAITING

Death is on the road, and death and anguish fill the sky, land, and sea, because men have never understood that the Brotherhood-of-Man principle is *LAW*, not a theoretical idealistic statement.

Our daily papers, radio, and television, tell their stories of human tragedy, and the world at large *knows not what to do with its problems.*

What is the *real* reason man knows not what to do with his problems? The answer is simple, and so very clear. As I stated previously, the *hardest* lesson we ever have to learn is that *the only thing that Life can give to us is that which we first gave to it.*

161

You may wonder *how* this statement applies to the dreadful death toll on the roads where innocent people are killed by careless and drunken drivers. Also why innocent people are drawn into wars, not of their own making, and killed, and *why* many crimes are committed where the victims of these crimes have had no prior personal contact with the criminals involved in the crimes.

To understand *fully* the answer to these inner questionings, one must *first* understand *how* we are all *one,* and how and why in this great Play of Creation we are all interdependent upon each other. Until we do understand these invisible laws, we shall *continue* to create tragedies such as those we read about in our daily newspapers. You will perhaps remember the heart-rending story where a young husband was rushing his wife, in labor of childbirth, to the hospital, and had a head-on collision with another car which injured his wife, who gave birth only to lose the baby and her young life because of the injury. Then there was the story of the distraught mother who knew intuitively when she heard of the accident to a little boy with a bicycle that it was her own little son. When her husband located their little one in a hospital, he was already dead. And then the short-lived joy of the honeymoon couple speeding to their honeymoon cottage—full of love and happiness one moment, and then the deadening silence of death the next. When these people died, part of all of us died with them.

162

Could these accidents have been avoided? Perhaps. So very many that happen *could* be avoided if only people thought *first* of others, instead of their own selfish sensations.

Thinking of others has almost become extinct in the twentieth century.

All over the world one hears the remark, *"The only thing Americans think of is the almighty dollar."* We know that this is not true of *all* Americans. I, for one, have found Americans to be loving, kind, and generous to a fault; but I have also found that many *do* place the emphasis on *money*, rather than on *character*.

Is it not time that we face ourselves with the truth and admit that for far too long we have been creating and living in an AGE OF MATERIALISM?

It would take too much space to explain HOW the seed of killing and greed for money and power has been ingrained into mankind's pattern of thinking, but it *is* this very seed-pattern which daily unfolds in the *thinking* of the human race. *As the know-how to weave a web is in the seed-pattern of a spider, so is the seed-pattern to kill within man himself.* Man has been sowing the seeds of killing and greed into the pattern of his seed for thousands of years. Only a recognition of his true Self will reverse his thinking, and replace *HATE* with *LOVE*.

Man has *taken* what he wants by the power of might-over-right practices for so long, but he has yet

Love

to learn that he will never hold that which he takes
by force. Balancing his actions may be a matter of
time, but they must—and always will—be balanced.

In our book entitled, *Scientific Answer to Human Relations,* we explain explicitly *how* and *why*
the slave will always arise and slay the master. No
man or nation can hold monopoly forever.

We foretold the present racial conflict in the
above-mentioned book in 1951. In our book, *The
World Crisis,* released in 1958, we warned of the
decline of the West, unless there was a reversal in
human relations. We stated that, unless *each race
lives* the Brotherhood-of-Man Law, *each will destroy
the other.*

We have reached the climax in the most crucial
period of this civilization. Man has the choice of
doing those things that will bring *balance* to his
human relations, or destroying the high peak of
technological advancement by his unbalanced takings. Desiring something for nothing has become too
great a part of man's thinking. This thinking is the
result of man's non-comprehension of the inviolate
law of Rhythmic Balanced Interchange. When man
at long last understands this law, and gives loving
service without thought of what he can get, there will
be abundance for all. As in *every* human transaction, if we desire to retain balance, we must *give and
be regiven equally,* for only in so doing do we fulfill
the Law of Balance which governs every man and
every nation on earth.

164

The Vital Role of Today's Youth

That is *why* scientific knowledge of man, himself, must be the *first* requisite of every man's education. All of the technological knowledge is *valueless* if we do not have worldwide peaceful interchange.

The role of every teen-ager, as well as of every *thinking* person, is to so live that only *balance* is expressed in every interchange between individuals and all peoples on earth. Peace will *never* come to any man, any community, any town or city, any country, or to the world, until man comprehends the fact that the basic *cause of every human agony* is his violation of the inviolate Law of Balance. It will take the great personal effort of every man and woman to fulfill completely this Law of Balance. We need each other, whether our skin is white, black, brown, yellow, or red. *We are all an equal extension of Creation.* Our lack of *awareness* of our true Selves is the *only* thing which separates us.

Remember, always, when you take the first step to give yourself to that which you want, it will take its first step to give itself to you. The whole universe is a mirror which reflects back to you that which you reflect forward into it, and LOVE, which all men desire, is like unto the ascent of a mountain. It comes ever nearer to you as you go ever nearer to it.

Your role in the great Play of Creation can give birth to a New Age of Character.

CHAPTER IX

On Building a Bright New Age
of Character

Laotzu, the great Chinese philosopher, said: *"If you want to go a thousand miles take the first step."* Many people have asked me what can be done, and what they can do, to help give birth to better times. I can think of no greater advice than that which Laotzu gave, and of no better way than beginning with ourselves. This we can do by putting into practice Natural Law in all of our interchangings and transactions.

Power is multiplied when many work together for a common cause, and what better cause is there than to build an *Age of Character*—because man's character creates his destiny.

In understanding our purpose on earth, and fulfilling the Law of Balance by living Natural Law, we shall give birth to a new era of *balanced progress*.

Cultural pursuits will feed our souls as well as our bodies. Creating *beauty* is profitable in every way. Man has not been fully *aware* of this fact, and has many times destroyed that which he most loved.

Swannanoa, our beautiful headquarters on Afton

Mountain in Virginia, was dedicated on May 2nd, 1949, for a world cultural center by the then President of the University of Virginia, Colgate W. Darden, Jr. Since that time, my late beloved husband and I completed a university curriculum of our new *Science of Man and Science of the Cosmos* teachings. Briefly I will give you an explanation of the purpose of our University, and a brief biography of ourselves.

THE UNIVERSITY OF SCIENCE AND PHILOSOPHY

Our University has been founded for the purpose of making a transition from sensing to knowing, by teaching students to *think and know,* instead of to *remember and repeat.* An education based solely upon reasoning through sensed-observation gradually undermines the power to think within, and tends toward the creating of a robot civilization.

Our University seeks to establish a balanced educational system in which *spiritual cause* is primary, and *physical effect* is secondary. Physical effect "educates" the senses only. The senses are limited to remembering all that is recorded on the brain for the purpose of repetition. In other words, the brain is not the Mind. We also seek to establish the import of man as being first in human values and relegate product and material values to their rightful place. Edwin Markham said: *"In vain do we build the city if we do not first build the man."*

167

Our University has been founded to enable man to transcend his sensed-thinking, by a gradual awakening of the power of Mind within, thus developing and intensifying his powers of creative expression. Our students are seekers of higher knowledge who are beginning to become aware of their inner powers, and to comprehend the difference between thinking and sensing. *Geniuses and super-geniuses do not think outwardly through their senses. They think inwardly through their Minds.*

All knowledge is lying dormant within every human being, but his awakening is slow. The geniuses and illuminates of the world are few. However, these few give all the cultural and spiritual progress to the world. They are the builders of great civilizations. The many, who are motivated by sensed-thinking, bring the agonies to the world through their might-over-right destructive practices.

WORLD'S GREAT NECESSITY

Alexis Carrel, noted scientist and author of *Man The Unknown,* once said that the world's great necessity was a university such as ours, a university which could give the knowledge men needed for the awakening of *the mighty power everyone has within himself,* instead of hopelessly seeking it outside of himself.

The teachings of our curriculum in the science of man and the science of the cosmos are filling the desires of many thousands of students who are becoming aware of their inner power.

168

On Building a Bright New Age of Character

Walter Russell's tremendous life exemplifies the mighty power which Alexis Carrel said all men had within them.

WALTER RUSSELL—THE MAN WHO TAPPED THE SECRETS OF THE UNIVERSE

A biographical story of this advanced mental stage, which is slowly coming to the whole human race, is briefly given in Glenn Clark's widely read book entitled, *The Man Who Tapped the Secrets of the Universe.* This book has deeply inspired many thousands of people, and given hope and courage to many who had felt handicapped because they did not have a college education.

My husband was forced to leave school at nine and a half years of age. His life was so fabulous that it seems almost incredible. He was official painter to President Theodore Roosevelt, official sculptor to President Franklin Delano Roosevelt, Architect, Composer, Author, Philosopher and Scientist. He was familiarly known as the modern Leonardo da Vinci, and the most versatile man in America. For more than sixty years he was listed in International Who's Who, and also in Who's Who in America.

The latter part of his long life was devoted to our University teachings, and to his scientific work and drawings. There are more than eighty of these scientific drawings included in our book entitled, *Atomic Suicide?* Dr. Russell refolded on his ninety-second birthday, May 19, 1963.

169

My husband was greatly concerned about the continued use of atomic fission, which he always claimed should not be used for war or industry. It was he who first made known to the world the existence of the two radioactive elements, which have become the basis of atomic energy, and the two hydrogen isotopes, which have become the basis of heavy water and the H-bomb. These he announced to the world of science in 1926, by copyrighted charts, under the names of *uridium* and *urium* for the nuclear fission elements, and *ethlogen* and *bebegen* for the hydrogen isotopes. Three years later, in 1929, the hydrogen elements were verified and renamed *deuterium* and *tritium*. Thirteen years later, in 1939, the transuranium elements were, likewise, verified and renamed *plutonium* and *neptunium*. In view of these documented facts, the reader can readily appreciate that such deep knowledge could only be given by one who has a thorough knowledge of Nature's ways and processes. It is this basic knowledge of what radioactivity is, and how it can destroy every vestige of life on this planet, which gives authority for the scientific statements in our book entitled, *Atomic Suicide?*

FORETOLD THE CALAMITIES FROM USE OF ATOMIC FISSION

My husband repeatedly stated that the continued use of atomic energy would so raise the temperature of the planet that the water levels all over the world would lower. We are today bearing witness to this fact. *The present serious water shortage, the increasing violence of tornadoes, hurricanes, and so many other things foretold in our book, Atomic Suicide? —published in 1957—have now become a reality.*

Many thinking people all over the world are now seriously reading *Atomic Suicide?*—and with ever-increasing understanding. This book scientifically explains the main *cause* of the water shortage, and other catastrophes, through the use of radioactive fission, with the *solution* to overcome them.

At no time in the history of our present civilization has man needed the worldwide cooperation of his fellow men as today. We are all in the same boat, relatively speaking, in regard to basic elemental needs. With unified effort we *shall* survive, and find that in and through each other we have always had that for which we fight and die to TAKE.

OUR UNITED PURPOSE

For fifteen years, we worked ceaselessly on our books together. We more often than not worked eighteen hours a day. Every moment of our lives had but one purpose, and that one purpose was to give to our fellow man that knowledge which had been given to us cosmically to aid mankind in this present crucial period of its unfolding.

LAO RUSSELL

My life has been dedicated to the transformation of world human relations. After losing my parents at the age of twelve and thirteen, my education was

Love

completed through private tutors. Remembering that my father always claimed that travel was the greatest education one could have, I traveled extensively to look into the hearts of men everywhere, to discover the *cause* of the many troubles and problems that had always beset man.

For several months I lived at the foot of the Great Pyramid of Giza, and during that period I journeyed across the Sahara Desert, where I found an eagerness for friendly sharing, and soon realized that people everywhere desired the same thing—*Love*. I found that all women liked to be admired for their beauty, and all men liked to possess and be admired for their power of leadership. The bartering of camels was done by man, and the work in the fields was done by the women.

In one camp that we visited in the desert, a young sixteen-year-old sixth wife of an old, toothless Bedouin Arab took me into her tent and, shyly taking down her veil, showed me how pretty she was. I could not speak Arabic, but with my eyes and hands I made it clear to her how very lovely I thought she was. The language of the eyes and heart have no language barriers.

I discovered that, geographically, it matters not where men and women are; all have the same basic desires—and the greatest desire of all is to love and to be loved.

I found that men and women for a period delude themselves into believing that *power* and *possessions* will satisfy their desires, but experiences usually

172

teach them—sometimes too late—that it was that elusive "something" man calls Love that they truly desired.

The greatest tragedy of man-in-the-mass is that he all too seldom understands what Love truly is, and mistakes his great sex drive for love only to become embittered when he finds it was not love but sex that held him prisoner.

In my journeyings and meetings with peoples of all races, I found few men and women who really understood their basic need of each other *mentally,* and that was why the world's thinking was *unbalanced.*

I came to the United States of America from England because it was a country I loved and admired, and the place I desired to make my home forever. And then destiny was fulfilled in my meeting with my beloved, and on July 29, 1948, we were married. Our oneness had but one great purpose, which was to demonstrate beauty, love, and balance.

Our first home was my husband's studio apartment in Carnegie Hall, New York. On November 1, 1948, we left New York to come to our mountaintop home at Swannanoa, Waynesboro, Virginia, where I created a Shrine of Beauty, and filled the great halls and rooms of the palace with my husband's great works of art and records of his illustrious life. The palace is also the headquarters of our Home-Study University.

Swannanoa was a ruin when we found it, and it

took much hard work to restore it to a condition where we could live in it, and open the main floor of the palace to the public. Electrical connections had to be installed, pipe repairs made to have water and heat, windows restored, door knobs replaced, and walls plastered. The grounds were a jungle. It was typical of any place left to the elements for fifteen odd years. For thirteen weeks I worked eighteen to twenty hours a day to make just a part of it livable. My husband worked on restoring sculptures he had in storage, and on completing numerous paintings; in addition, we wrote a book together—all in six months prior to our dedication opening. Now this lovely Shrine of Beauty is open to the public every day of the year.

Students journey thousands of miles to visit us. They have been doing so since the day of our dedication, May 2, 1949. They come, not only from the farthest corners of this country, but from all over the world.

Since our teachings are based solely upon Natural Law, they are not in variance with any religious beliefs and are, therefore, universally acceptable. We have people of all races, nationalities, and creeds, among our student body.

THE FULFILLMENT WHICH SATISFIES

We are on earth to fulfill the purpose of the Man Idea. Therefore, all that we do should be *purposeful*. When it is, we feel a sense of achievement.

174

Giving form to a creative idea brings a sense of *contentment*. This is because we are fulfilling ourselves by living purposefully. When money motive *alone* dominates, unbalanced by the sheer joy of creating, which is *giving* to life, we do not experience that feeling of fulfillment. The senses, alone, can never fully satisfy, for only Soul qualities bring complete fulfillment.

A true genius *has* to express himself. Time means nothing to him—neither does money. When Ossip Gabrilowitsch, the great musician and Director of the Detroit Symphony, was posing for my husband to sculpture his bust, my husband did not get that feeling of music in his features that he desired to portray. He asked Gabrilowitsch to play for him so that he could interpret a feeling of music, and Gabrilowitsch said, *"But how can I play for one person?"* My husband said to him, *"How many do you ever play for?"* He knew that a genius never really does anything except for *inner* fulfillment and satisfaction.

CHARACTER—OUR ONE GREAT PURPOSE

Character building is our one great purpose. All else is incidental and transitory. All material possessions are really *not* possessions; they are *things* we have the use of while we are on earth, but we cannot keep them forever. They are not a *permanent* part of us. And yet men sell their souls for a pot of gold, and wonder why they cannot gain the contentment they perpetually seek.

People's actions are measured by their awareness of what is *right* and what is *wrong*. However, all of us make mistakes under certain emotional conditions. At such times our judgment is unbalanced.

Every man is at a different stage of awareness. As every leaf on a tree is different, so is every man different in his thought processes. For this reason, one can understand *why* it is a great challenge for human beings to live in harmony with each other. The sooner we realize our deep need of each other, the sooner shall we work with and for each other.

FORGETTING SELF

HUMILITY is a most admirable quality. One always finds a great person easy to talk to because of his humbleness. Humility comes from forgetting self—the little self. It was the quality I most admired in my beloved husband—a master in so many fields, and yet, with it all, so truly humble. He would say there was a world of difference in man's little ego and his big ego—which is his higher Self. He *lived* this philosophy, and there was not *anything* he felt *beneath* his dignity to do.

I would like to share with you a few thoughts my husband expressed on *humility*. They were included in his **Five Laws of Success,** in Glenn Clark's magnificent biography of his life, entitled, *The Man Who Tapped the Secrets of the Universe*.

On Building a Bright New Age of Character

"No great man has ever wisecracked his way into greatness.

Until one learns to lose one's self he cannot find himself.

He must first divide himself and give himself to the service of all, thus placing himself within all others through acts of thoughtfulness and service.

The personal ego must be suppressed and replaced with the 'universal ego.' One must not be the part, one must be the whole. The 'I' must be forgotten. I had it. All men have it, and all pass through that stage.

I once thought that greatness was the only thing worthwhile, but when I achieved it to some extent I found that I was not satisfied with it, because there was something beyond, so much higher, that all publicity and praise made me feel ashamed instead of proud, for I felt there was so much farther to go than I had gone. Early in life I found that to achieve greatness one had to go only one inch beyond mediocrity, but that one inch is so hard to go that only those who become aware of God in them can make the grade, for no one can achieve that one inch alone.

When I arrived at the point where I received public acclaim I felt the most lowly, because I knew within myself that I had but begun to tap my inner resources. I knew that I had not yet achieved that one inch which would make of me a worthy messenger.

Love

No one can make a sale, write a book or invent anything without first having deep reverence which makes him know and feel that he is merely an interpreter of the thought-world, one who is creating a product of some kind to fit a purpose."

I know these words of my beloved will echo in the heart and Soul of every man who has touched the summit of his desires. Again, I say, when we truly touch the heights, we know our oneness with all life —and with God—and we cry out within ourselves for our other Selves.

COURAGE TO DO WHAT IS RIGHT

To champion a new cause takes *courage*. I never think of this word COURAGE that I do not think of what that courageous woman, Amelia Earhart, the great U. S. aviation pioneer who flew the Atlantic in a solo crossing in 1932, said of this quality, *"Courage is the price that life exacts for granting peace. The soul that knows it not, knows no release from little things."*

We need courage to do the *right* thing sometimes, even though it is often easier to do the wrong. A person will do the wrong thing because he cannot stand not being accepted, and must have a sense of "belonging." All people desire to "belong" to someone or something.

I believe everyone is basically good and kind. Therefore, for many, it is either a question of being *guided* in the right direction, or having the *courage* to do the *right* thing.

I have read of gangsters who are very kind and gentle to their mothers, or someone they love, and yet they will kill a man for a few dollars. If such people could only *comprehend* Natural Law, I believe they would use the intelligence they have to good advantage. It is not even intelligently selfish to kill and rob, for anyone who breaks the law knows that he can never freely enjoy his ill-gotten gain. With the constant fear of being caught, there can never be a sense of freedom, inner peace, and happiness. Through his desires and actions man inflicts joy or sorrow upon himself and upon his fellow man.

THE REVOLT OF NATURE

In our book, *The One-World Purpose*—which my husband and I wrote together in 1960—we have one chapter entitled, **The Day of Reckoning. The Revolt of Nature Against Man Law Because of Man Revolt Against Natural Law.** That day is now *here*.

When we wrote this chapter, there were worldwide tragedies constantly occurring—as there are today —wherein young people were committing appalling crimes against innocent victims, such as gangs of young hoodlums descending on innocent groups and beating them up for no reason at all. Then there were, and still are, the unbelievable crimes of youths killing their parents on slight provocations, such as not being allowed to use the family car, etc.

A news commentator said recently that, unless the present rate of crime ceased, it would not be safe to walk on our streets after dark in five years' time.

When we foretold such incidents, in *The One-World Purpose,* we knew that many people thought we were "far out." Today, many people are aware that it is not safe to be on many of the streets in big cities after dark—or even during the day. This same condition is spreading out to communities all over the United States, and abroad, also.

As I write this book, the riots in Los Angeles are flaring; people are uselessly being killed and injured, and no real solution is found. To police our streets with armed guards is not the permanent solution. The great tragedy is that the basic underlying *cause* of these violent outbreaks is not understood.

It is imperative that all people become aware of the *cause* of our dilemma, so that we can have a realistic approach to our present-day problems. This solution must be based on the scientific laws of the universe. For centuries, man has ruled by the principle of *might*-over-right. The time is now *here* when only by living the law of *right*-over-might will peace be brought to any country. *ALL* countries *must* recognize this principle if our world is to survive.

Governing bodies, everywhere, must come to the

realization that, unless the desire of Soul to give love out from itself is fulfilled, the body will react by demanding physical sensations in varied immoral excesses.

We can only stop the little and big gang wars of hate by each and every one of us living the Law of Love. It will take great courage, and much self-discipline, but the rewards will be personal contentment and peace for all mankind.

We shall find that as we live love—which means *giving service*—that we shall be happier than we have ever been before. And as we become happier, ourselves, our family, neighbors and friends, will reflect this happiness.

WE ALL NEED EACH OTHER

As you become more and more aware of your basic and powerful potential, you will know the ecstasy of Mind-knowing. Then all things of your body, which give but transitory sensation, will take their rightful place, and not be the stumbling blocks which they have been.

Remember, always, that YOU are the world, and the world is YOU. As *you* think and act, so will the whole world.

Every man IS his brother's keeper. Whatever your position or work in life is, YOU are important to every other man. There is no position that can take this importance away from you. Whether you run the elevator to the head executive's office, or whether you sit at that desk, *you are important to each other*.

This brings to mind the story my husband used to tell of his conversation with the elevator man who was taking him to see Thomas Edison, to whom my husband was official sculptor.

The man remarked, *"Mr. Edison is a great man. I am just an elevator man."* My husband said to him, *"Every man is a great man when he is fulfilling a purpose. If you did not take Mr. Edison up these many floors in your elevator, Mr. Edison could not sit at his desk."*

When we recognize our *need* of each other, we work *with* each other.

YOUTH'S GREAT CHALLENGE TO CREATE A NEW AGE OF CHARACTER

Youth is a time for progressive thinking, acting, and growing. Working constructively with Natural Law, you can give birth to a bright New Age. You have a clean slate on which to draw your blueprint for a world united in loving service of man to man.

You can mentally start this very moment to begin to create an Age of Character, and unfold the inner power of your own potential. The power of Mind is not limited to body actions. It reaches out to all the world, and to the farthermost star in the heavens.

Equip yourself with the scientific knowledge of man and the cosmos. Live Natural Law without compromise, and the power of the whole, *limitless* space of eternity is yours.

Knowledge—and all of the invisible qualities of Mind—must be *earned,* as all things of the material world must also be earned. *There is no substitute for work.* Work means *effort,* and not anything can come to you without great effort. The greater the effort, the greater the accomplishment. As my beloved husband said: *"Genius is self-bestowed and Mediocrity is self-inflicted."* Thomas Edison put it this way: *"Genius is one per cent inspiration and ninety-nine per cent perspiration."* Every man who has accomplished great things has always done so by sheer hard work.

The world has grown dark with *FEAR.* Only *LOVE* can *void* that *FEAR. It has to be love in action. Words,* alone, will not help. Working together, with love, toward the single purpose of a better way of life, we cannot fail to give birth to the greatest age ever known in the history of mankind—an AGE OF CHARACTER.

FINALE

And now we say to you, do not be confused with the complexities of life. When life seems complex, and you have decisions to make because of these complexities, remember this one thing: You have only one simple decision to make at this moment—only one. The next one has not yet arrived.

That one decision you must make is that you shall do only that which makes you loved. There is no decision other than that which any man may make and find happiness for himself and give happiness to the world.

Upon that one principle a great civilization once lived in which crime, fear, hate, and greed, were never known. That civilization did not have one policeman or soldier, for there was no need of them. Each man was trained from childhood to do only that which would make him loved. *May the day come again when man shall do only that which will make him to be loved.*

—From Walter and Lao Russell's *Home Study Course in Universal Law. Natural Science and Living Philosophy*

Lao and Dr. Walter Russell at the Kiwanis Club in Salem, Virginia, where they filled a lecture engagement.

Lao and Dr. Walter Russell starting on their daily walk
around the mountain.

Dr. Walter and Lao Russell directing the preparation of the mold for casting their colossal statue of the Christ of the Blue Ridge. This statue was conceived by the author and sculptured by both Walter and Lao Russell.

Lao Russell beside the bust of her late beloved husband,
Dr. Walter Russell, which they sculptured together.

The author and her late husband, Dr. Walter Russell, at one of his birthday parties. The two background pictures are drawings by Walter Russell when he was war artist and correspondent for *Collier's* and *Century* in the Spanish-American War.

A candid picture at a birthday party for the author.

Lao Russell and her beloved husband, Dr. Walter Russell. The pastel portraits behind them are the maternal grandparents of the author.

The beautiful gardens at Swannanoa with sculptural works of Walter and Lao Russell.

Part III

"The dawn telleth the coming of the new day.
I turn my eyes to the morning and purge myself
in the purity of the dawn.

My Soul quickeneth with the beauty of the
dawn.

Today is, and will be.

Yesterday was, and has been.

My yesterday is what I made it. I see it in
memory, perfect or imperfect.

My today is what I will to make it.

I will to make it perfect."

—From "Salutation to the Day,"
by WALTER RUSSELL

CHAPTER X

International Age of Character Clubs

The sole purpose of the International Age of Character Clubs is to give people of every race, nationality, and creed, and in every walk in life, an opportunity to share that greatest joy on earth—*interchange with loving understanding.*

This loving interchange will come to all peoples when they comprehend their true purpose on earth, their true relationship with each other, and with their Creator.

To fill the desires and needs of people of all ages, *cultural and sports activities* will be a part of the PROGRAM OF EVENTS of the clubs. These activities are necessary, not only for the building of character, but also for the building of understanding among all peoples of the world toward each other.

For almost twenty years, groups of our students have been forming in practically every country in the world. They gather together periodically to discuss our teachings, and in their discussions they clarify their own thinking and multiply their understanding in and through each other, as well as experiencing the deep joys of sharing with those of like thinking.

Getting together for sessions of discussion and study gives one a whole new incentive for living *creatively*. The stimulation of being with others of like thinking opens whole new vistas of thought which give birth to creative ideas. We all need this stimulation which creates within us a more joyous attitude to life. This joyousness attracts that special "someone" to us with whom we can share ourselves.

Romances bloom and blossom in these groups, and many marriages occur with lasting success because of a common meeting of Mind, which forever keeps the physical vibrantly alive.

With the ever-increasing desire of new students for introductions to other students in their area, I thought it well to inform old and new readers and students that officially we will call our groups the *INTERNATIONAL AGE OF CHARACTER CLUBS*.

NEED FOR GROWTH INTO CULTURAL AND SPORTS ACTIVITIES

The time has come when many activities should be added to our student group meetings.

These International Age of Character Clubs create a desire for universal cooperation, and give the opportunity for expression of latent desires in the creative arts, crafts, and sports.

Working on creative ideas *together* increases enthusiasm to excel in creative expression. Finding one's self excelling in painting, sculpturing, writing, ceramics, woodwork, or any other creative art, brings a great sense of well-being and immense inner satisfaction. Often when our students start sculpturing, they are amazed at what they can do.

EVERYONE CAN DO "SOMETHING"

Lack of funds will not keep anyone from participating in the many cultural and sports activities. These clubs will be within the reach of all.

A SPECIAL MESSAGE TO OUR STUDENTS

We especially call upon those of our students who have expressed their desire to help to write us in regard to forming new local groups for membership in the International Age of Character Clubs. There is something for everyone to do—and the time is NOW.

You will find that local authorities will be happy and willing to work *with* you when you explain the purpose and objective of these Clubs. The need for a *united* purpose to bring balance, harmony, and good will, toward our neighbors has become a *necessity* in practically every community in our country, and in every country in the world.

Your local newspapers, radio, and television stations, will be happy to cooperate with you. Cooperation creates interest. Increased interest means increased business for local tradespeople. It is the best type of promotion for any and all business interchangings.

In every community there is usually a building—or part of a building—that could be used to start a Club; and since such a Club as the International Age of Character Club is for everyone's benefit, people will desire to contribute their time and their substance in many ways.

Local Clubs can add many cultural and sports activities as they grow in membership and have the necessary funds for operation.

SOCIAL GATHERINGS AND LECTURES

This spring I gave twenty-one lectures in the Midwest and West, and had the great joy of meeting hundreds of our students. Part of every year's schedule is to visit periodically and give talks to country-wide students and members, and also European and other countries where our International Age of Character Clubs are formed. Also, to attend special events where awards will be given to winning contestants in the arts and crafts, and in sports competitions.

STUDENTS' CHRISTMAS GATHERINGS AT SWANNANOA

Last Christmas we had a wonderful four-day gathering at Swannanoa, our University of Science and Philosophy headquarters. Student members came from all parts of the country, and are eagerly looking forward to attending these Christmas reunions yearly. Those attending ranged from professional men and women to housewives and teen-agers.

The beautiful letters that came from those who attended our Christmas Gathering filled our hearts with gratitude. Each letter contained a great regiving of love and appreciation. I would like to share *all* of them with you. However, these few quotations will tell you of the deep love that emanated from all who were here, and how those present took the warmth of Christmas Love and spirit back into their workaday world.

"Dear Lao Russell,

'Stepping in the light'—Oh, so beautiful it was to walk into the Palace of Light and Beauty—and feel ourselves warmed by the radiance of your love—and that of other great souls gathered there—An experience we shall forever treasure! . . .

We saw the most elaborate lighting displays in homes along the way—But what I keep remembering is that most glorious light we found there— in your face—as you gave us the secret for carrying Christmas into every day. . . .

I do so want to keep myself a clear channel for God's love to come through—in all the areas busy living leads me. There is such tremendous need for love—everywhere. People who care are so needed!

It was such a mountain-top experience being there

199

—being recharged (yes getting our run-down batteries re-charged, that's it) and getting fortified for meeting the ever-increasing challenge of living in today's world. You told us it would not be easy coming down. How very wise you are—and practical. I'll have to tell you this . . . The trip back, P. and I felt so wonderfully close in spirit—reliving and sharing all the precious moments and learning experiences that had been ours. God's Hand was at the wheel with each of us as we took turns driving. But it was a long trip (over 400 miles) and quite late (2:00 A.M.) when we got in . . . and slipped ourselves into bed to sleep blissfuly. . . . E. & P. W."

"Dear Lao,

Your wonderful gift of love breaks down all artificial barriers and makes us conscious of our oneness in God. I don't know how to thank you enough for opening up your heart and your home to those of us who came to be with you at Christmas. It was an experience truly to be cherished and one I know I will never forget. . . . Mr. B. M."

"My Dear Lao,

Although it will take a few days for me to regain balance and tune myself to the discord of this very much outer living. The thoughts and ecstasy of our Christmas will join me again in my moments of meditation, that oneness, love and understanding can be relived everyday.

Only those who experienced these exquisite days, when time completely vanished to be replaced by balance, harmony and Love.

It proved how strangers seeking knowledge, understanding and oneness can have also balanced rhythmic interchange . . . Mr. P. P."

"Dear, dear Lao,

Back home again, after a sacred memorable Christmas with you and beloved seekers after Truth!

Thank you—thank you—thank you—Lao, for this time of deep, tender and poignant sharing with you!

Whenever I play Stokowski's orchestral rendition of the Love-Death theme of Tristan and Isolde— that heart-piercing, unearthly haunting music of Wagner, the illuminate—I shall think, brood and meditate over your own *liebestoide—the deathless love that was yours and your beloved's.*

Since love is the mainspring of life and since life gives birth to death and death springs forth into life —nothing—nothing—can ever separate the two of you! What a glorious hope! What a tremendous knowing! . . .

I shall play the Tristan and Isolde music now, listening with a deeper understanding and it will be a mystical, unwritten form of communication between us. Bless you. Miss B. W."

Love

"Lao, my dearest One,

What better way could I begin the New Year of 1965 than writing to you?

What words can I write that will express the great ecstasy or elation which fills my heart since I met you?

I think you know that I have been looking for you all my life. You, the someone who understands my heart.

Thank you for inviting me to Swannanoa. I have never experienced such a beautiful Christmas or any other time.

Your wonderful talks with us, the heavenly music, the warm loving fellowship of all present, the beautiful decorations, your lovely refreshments.

The opportunity of strolling off by one's self and closely observing the great works of your beloved, and last but not the least, your own wonderful self. So radiant with divine love, so inspiring to each of us present, so full of love for all of us that we felt our hearts burn within us.

Thank you, for your goodbye to me. I cherish each word spoken by you, each loving smile. The memory of it will live in my heart. Mrs. M. E. G."

WEDDING BELLS

The writer of the above letter has just telephoned telling me that she is going to marry a wonderful man whom she met here at our last year's Christmas party. They will be married at our beautiful Swannanoa Palace this Christmas Eve. Is not this a lovely

202

story of a "prince" and "princess" who found their dreams of romance come true because they knew and lived the law of love?

The above excerpts from letters are typical of all the letters from those who shared our Christmas joys, and also of all letters that come from our students who are so aware of the Light of Love which centers all mankind awaiting its awakening.

This is the Love that you will find extended to you through your local International Age of Character Clubs. You can never know loneliness when you have those who understand to share your joys and your sorrows. Your local clubs provide the ideal place for meeting others who think and feel about the high ideals of life as you do. We all need someone with whom we can share our thoughts.

The International Age of Character Clubs, and the extension of our teachings in the Science of Man and the Science of the Cosmos, have but one basic purpose, and that purpose is to help you know your true Self, your relationship to your Creator, and your relationship to your fellow man. When you comprehend these things, you will understand your purpose on earth, and desire to fulfill it.

Let this be your new day when you take that first step to the horizon of your desire. Fulfill your individual role and purpose in the great drama of Life—THE PLAY OF CREATION!

INTERNATIONAL AGE OF
CHARACTER CLUB
PLEDGE FOR MEMBERSHIP

The *ONE* pledge to become a member
of this club is:

*"I WILL DO ONLY THAT WHICH
MAKES ME LOVED."*

For complete information for MEMBERSHIP
in the International Age of Character Clubs
address inquiries as follows:

International Age of Character Club,
University of Science and Philosophy,
Swannanoa,
Waynesboro, Virginia,
U. S. A.

No membership dues are charged by the
University of Science and Philosophy

YOUR LOVE BANK

Somewhere beyond that blue horizon, the one you seek is seeking you. Love and life triumphant is your divine heritage. True Love is everyone's inheritance from Life. Every day of your life you are building a large or small deposit of Love in the Bank of Life.

Every thought is deposited (recorded) and every action is deposited (recorded). This is not just a fairy story. *This is a scientific fact.*

Everyone's thoughts and actions are permanently recorded. Therefore, see that *your* "deposits" are made up of the qualities you desire to find reflected in your sweetheart. In this way you will build a "fortune" for balanced matehood.

Open *your* bank account today, and tomorrow the deepest desire of your heart and life shall be *your very own*.

UNIVERSITY OF SCIENCE AND PHILOSOPHY, SWANNANOA, WAYNESBORO, VIRGINIA

A LETTER TO YOU FROM ME

Dear, dear Reader:

I would like to look into your eyes, and tell you in person all these things I have endeavored to explain simply to you about LOVE and SEX. I *know* your desire for Love and Happiness. It is an age-old one, and one for which man has sought throughout his continual life cycles. He can never stop seeking it, for it ever remains his goal.

This is a sexed-electric universe; and all too few realize or comprehend that organic, as well as inorganic, beings and things are governed by the sex principle. Without the rains from Father-heavens, we could not have the produce from the womb of Mother-earth. It is the constant interchange between the two that gives us food to sustain our bodies. This *must* be a *balanced* interchange to give birth to the produce that feeds us. This same *balanced* sex principle for utility purposes is illustrated in the lock and key. One without the other is valueless.

You can find countless illustrations of the sex principle in every department of life. This is fully explained all through our teachings in the Science of Man and the Science of the Cosmos. When you understand this principle, you will better understand your physical desires and drives. You will learn to balance your physical desires with your mental and spiritual ones. In this balance, you will find the key to your sustained happiness. Most importantly, as you find yourself happy *within,* you will attract to yourself happiness from *without* in the form of your perfect mate. Love attracts love. It cannot fail to do so, for Love is *all* there is in this great and beautiful world of ours.

Bless you, and may this book help you to find that one true love your heart desires.

Lovingly yours,